DIRECTOR'S CHOICE

LEEDS MUSEUMS AND GALLERIES

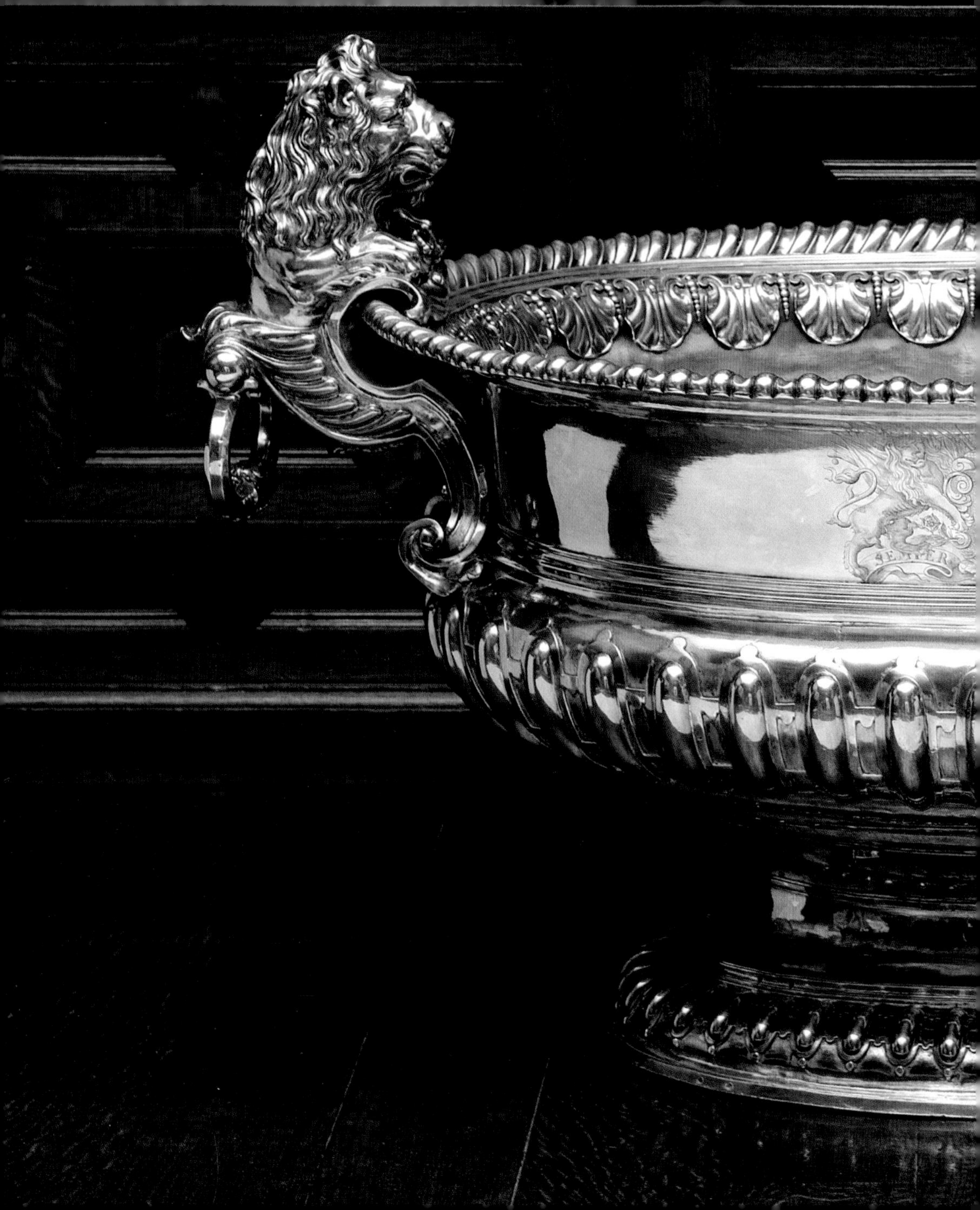

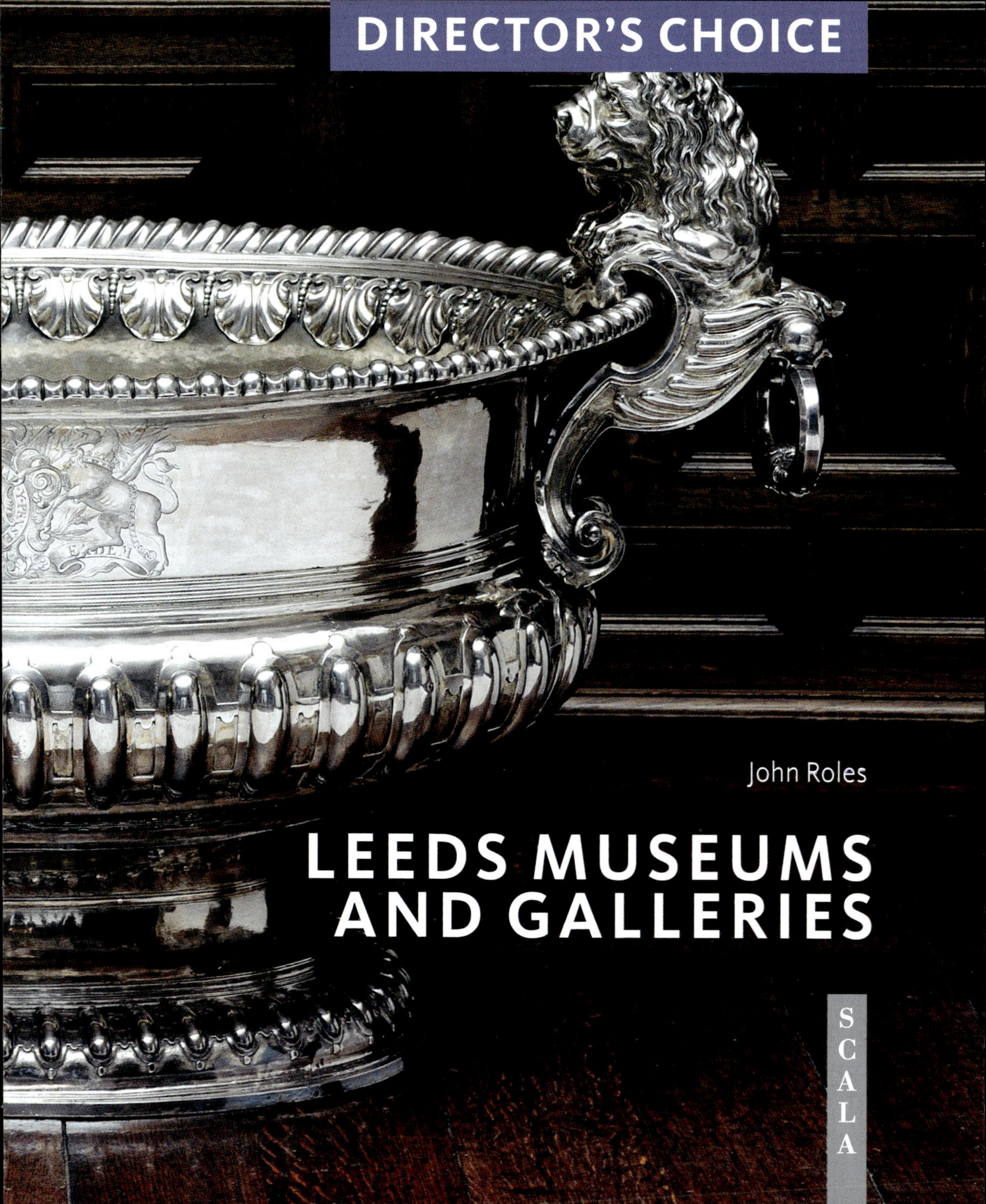
DIRECTOR'S CHOICE
John Roles
LEEDS MUSEUMS AND GALLERIES
SCALA

INTRODUCTION

Leeds has a museum tradition stretching back to the antiquarian Ralph Thoresby's private *Musaeum Thoresbyanum* in the seventeenth century. But the origins of the modern museum lie with The Leeds Philosophical and Literary Society who founded the Leeds Philosophical Hall in Park Row in 1821. The original building soon proved inadequate for the rapidly growing collections of natural history, geology and antiquities, so in the 1860s the building was demolished and a new structure, twice the size, replaced it. Soon afterwards, a campaign to build a civic art gallery was under way. Using the occasion of the Queen's jubilee in 1887, a public subscription was raised to support a number of competing projects. The establishment of an art gallery won out and Leeds Art Gallery opened its doors in 1888.

It wasn't until 1921 that the Society gifted the museum and its collections to the Leeds Corporation, which precipitated the growth of the city's museums to the number and variety we know today. The Temple Newsam estate was purchased in 1922; Abbey House Museum opened in 1927, followed by Kirkstall Abbey (1954); Lotherton Hall was presented by the Gascoigne Family in 1968; Armley Mills opened in 1969 and in 1990 Thwaite Mills joined the service. The city museum on Park Row finally closed in 1966, having been severely damaged in 1941, and the collections moved to what is now the Central Library. It was to be another four decades before the museum had a new home of its own, with the opening in September 2008 of the Leeds City Museum, along with the Discovery Centre.

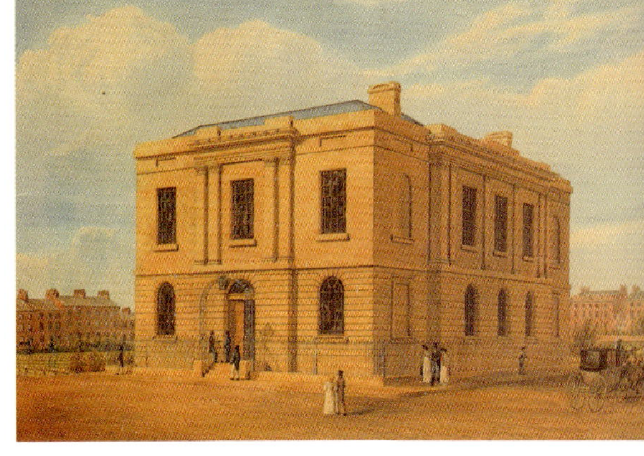

Leeds Philosophical Hall, 1822

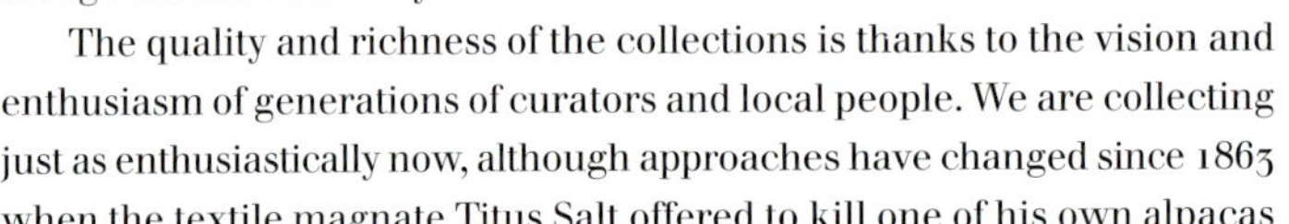

The quality and richness of the collections is thanks to the vision and enthusiasm of generations of curators and local people. We are collecting just as enthusiastically now, although approaches have changed since 1863 when the textile magnate Titus Salt offered to kill one of his own alpacas

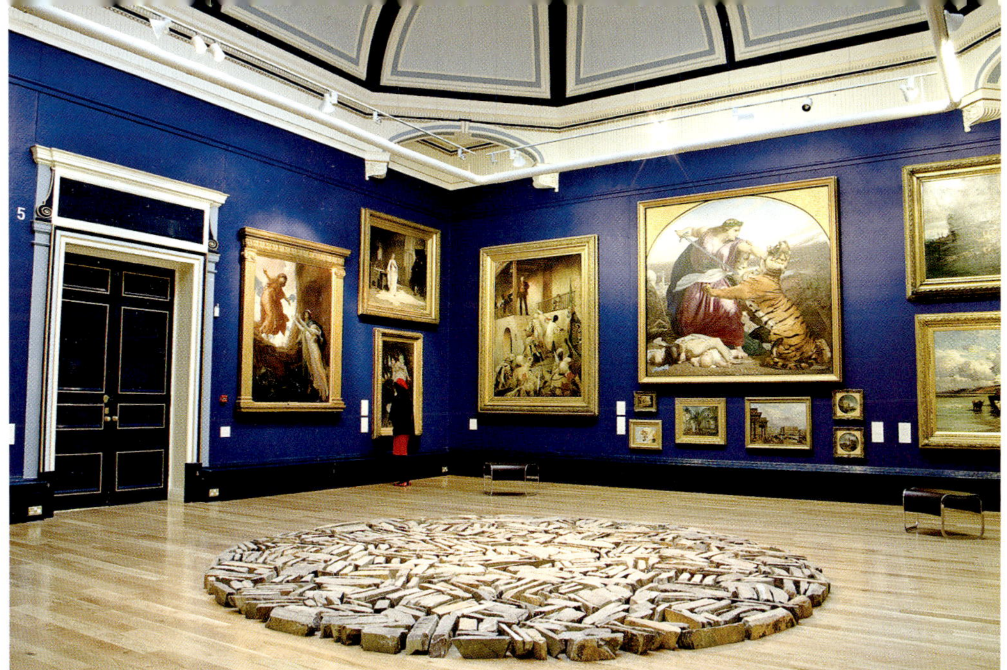

Leeds Art Gallery, 2010

for the museum collection – an offer that was accepted, with members sitting down in the Queens Hotel to enjoy a meal of the alpaca before the poor creature's pelt and bones were recovered for the museum.

Making a selection from such a vast range has not been easy, but it has been a pleasure: having reason to spend time with curators, discussing collections and renewing relations with pieces I, all too often, rush past between meetings. The debates were stimulating and the inevitable competition to make the final cut was bloody. Drawing just a few from so very many treasures proved almost impossible, something like the challenge of choosing one's Desert Island Discs. What I have drawn together are some standout pieces, many telling us something of Leeds as a major industrial city and almost all saying something about our civilisation or our environment.

So here is my selection. I hope it is representative of the highlights and includes some unexpected gems; and I hope that amongst my choices you find some of your own personal favourites. But above all I hope it will inspire you to visit our sites to enjoy some of the finest collections amongst the best museums and galleries in the country.

The Sognefjord, c.1885

ADELSTEEN NORMANN, 1848–1918

Oil on canvas, 213.5 × 320 cm

Gift from Colonel T. R. Harding, 1890

LEEAG.1890.77

LEEDS ART GALLERY opened in October 1888, as an extension to the Municipal Buildings. A 30-year campaign by several single-minded individuals, spearheaded by Col. Walter Harding, was waged to create a civic gallery for Leeds. Great paintings by leading artists of the day were expensive and funds for acquisitions were not assured. The founding collection was modest, comprising gifts to the city since 1858, but it formed the kernel of what was to become one of the most revered civic art collections in the UK.

This picture, the magnificent *Sognefjord* by Adelsteen Normann was one of the early gifts from Colonel Thomas Harding, Walter's father. Taking opportunities to buy great art of the moment has always characterised the Leeds collection and this is possibly the earliest example. The Royal Academy Summer Exhibition provided a source for new art. Works unsold in London often travelled to art fairs around the country afterwards, in the hope of finding buyers. This was one such work and it was snapped up by Harding at the Leeds Spring Exhibition and presented to the gallery. He followed this with several more gifts and sums of money for future acquisitions.

The picture itself is a dramatic centrepiece of the Ziff Gallery of historical pictures. The subject is probably the 'Naeroyfjord', an arm of the Sognefjord, the deepest and one of the longest fjords in the world. It is one of several large canvases by this artist that emphasised the drama of the Norwegian landscape which were widely exhibited in many major European cities. It was a significant acquisition at the time and has been hugely popular with visitors to the gallery ever since. It was recently voted one of *Yorkshire's Favourite Paintings* in a public campaign.

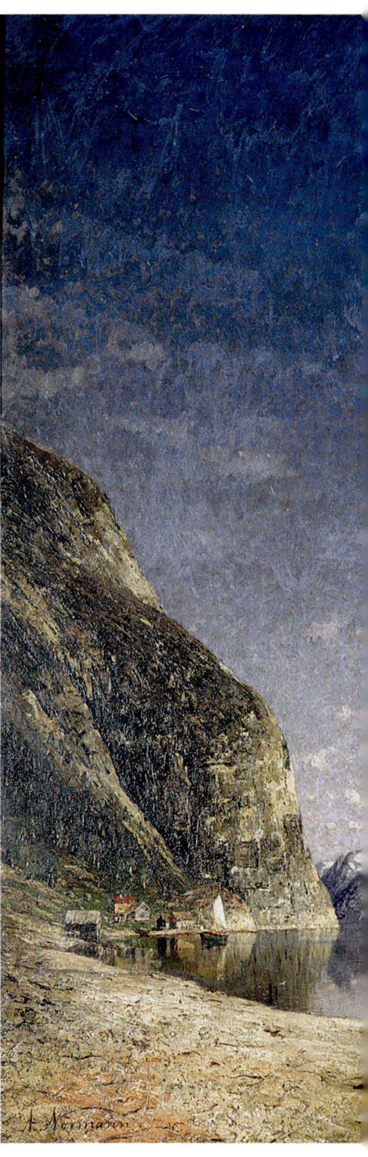

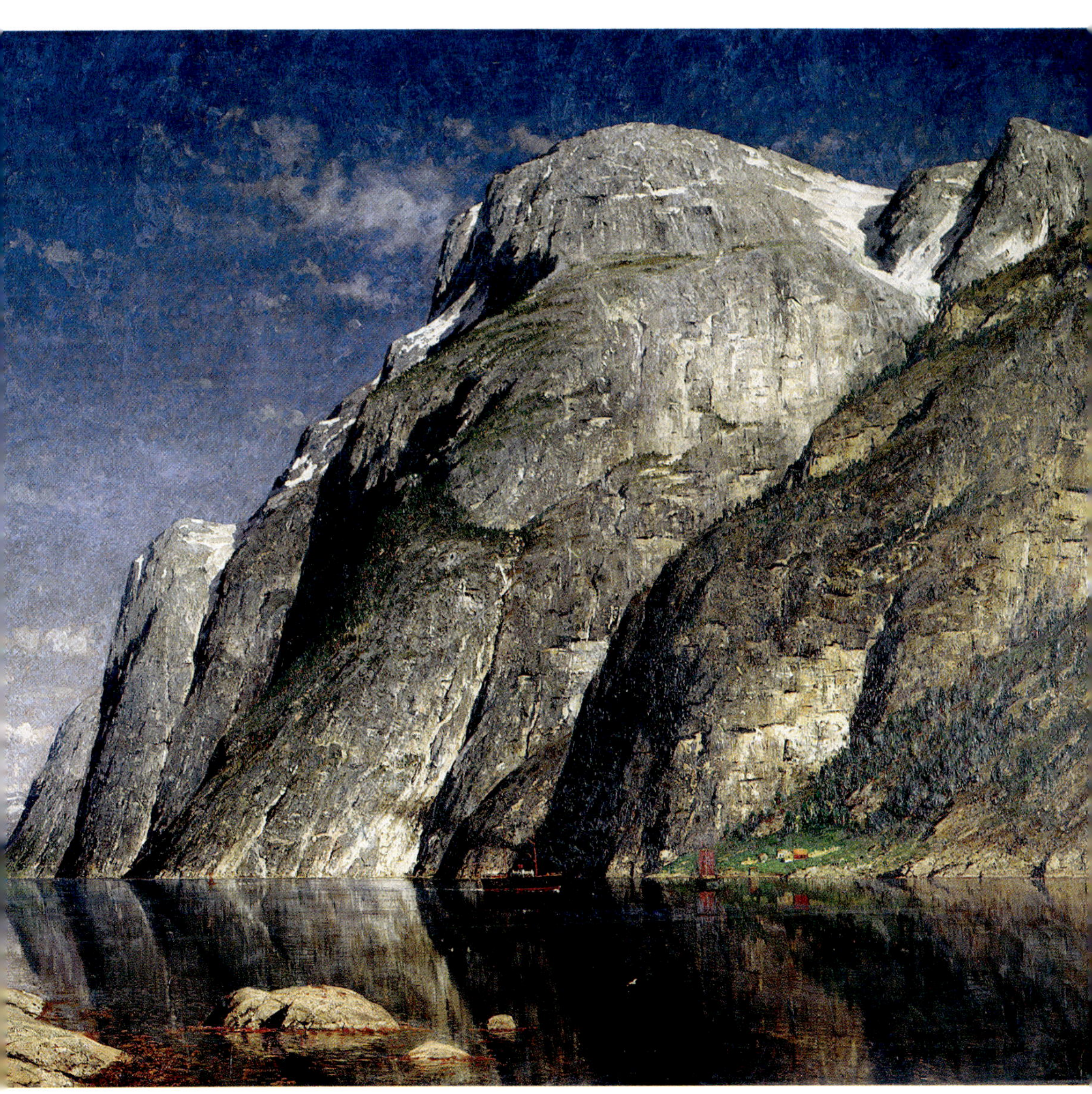

The Day of Atonement, 1919

Jacob Kramer, 1892–1962

Oil on canvas, 99 × 121.9 cm

Gift from the Jewish Community of Leeds, 1920

LEEAG.1920.276

The early twentieth century was a vibrant period in British art and for the Leeds art collections. 'Modern art' was taking hold and artists influenced by political and societal upheaval began to challenge traditional academic practice. Amid the roll call of Slade School of Art alumni of this period – Stanley Spencer, Walter Sickert, Charles Ginner – the Leeds artist Jacob Kramer was emerging as a new talent from the Leeds and Slade schools of Art.

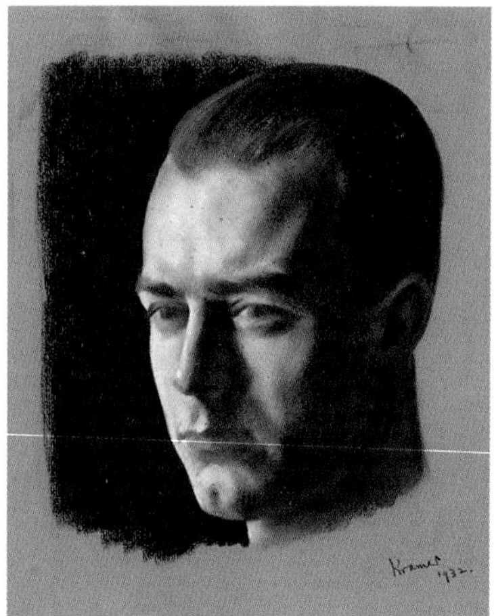

Kramer arrived in Leeds as a child with his family, having fled the rise of anti-Semitism in the Ukraine. A promising talent, he became involved with the radical Leeds Art Club where he developed ideas of depicting the spiritual dimension through painting. He earned his fame in London and returned to Leeds in the 1920s, this time as something of a local celebrity. He was instrumental in bringing leading cultural figures to address the Yorkshire Luncheon Club held at Whitelock's public house.

One of his key works is the startling *The Day of Atonement*. Commissioned by the Leeds Jewish Representative Council as a gift to Leeds Art Gallery, it represents Yom Kippur, the holiest day in the Jewish calendar. A deeply moving depiction of a procession of Jewish scholars, wearing their prayer shawls and walking in silent prayer, it displays a strong Vorticist influence. At the time of the gift it was the most modern painting in a collection of mostly Victorian and Edwardian pictures.

Alas, Kramer's success and wealth didn't last. Back in Leeds he became an alcoholic and was reduced to producing sketch portraits – often of mixed quality – to pay for his drinks. One particular portrait stands out for me – of the future Leeds Galleries Director Ernest Musgrave (shown above). One of my predecessors, he would later become a significant driving force for the galleries.

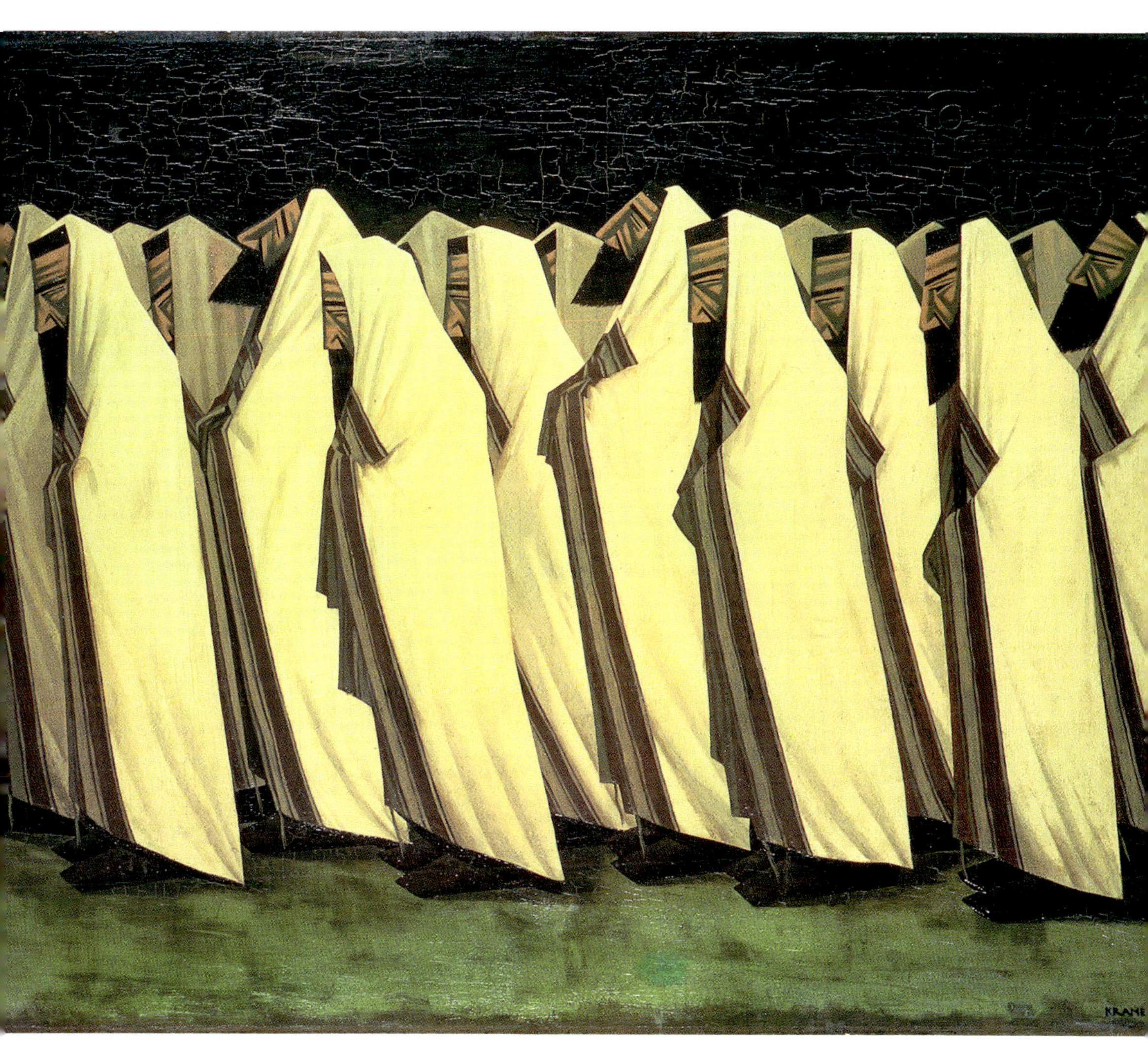
KRANE

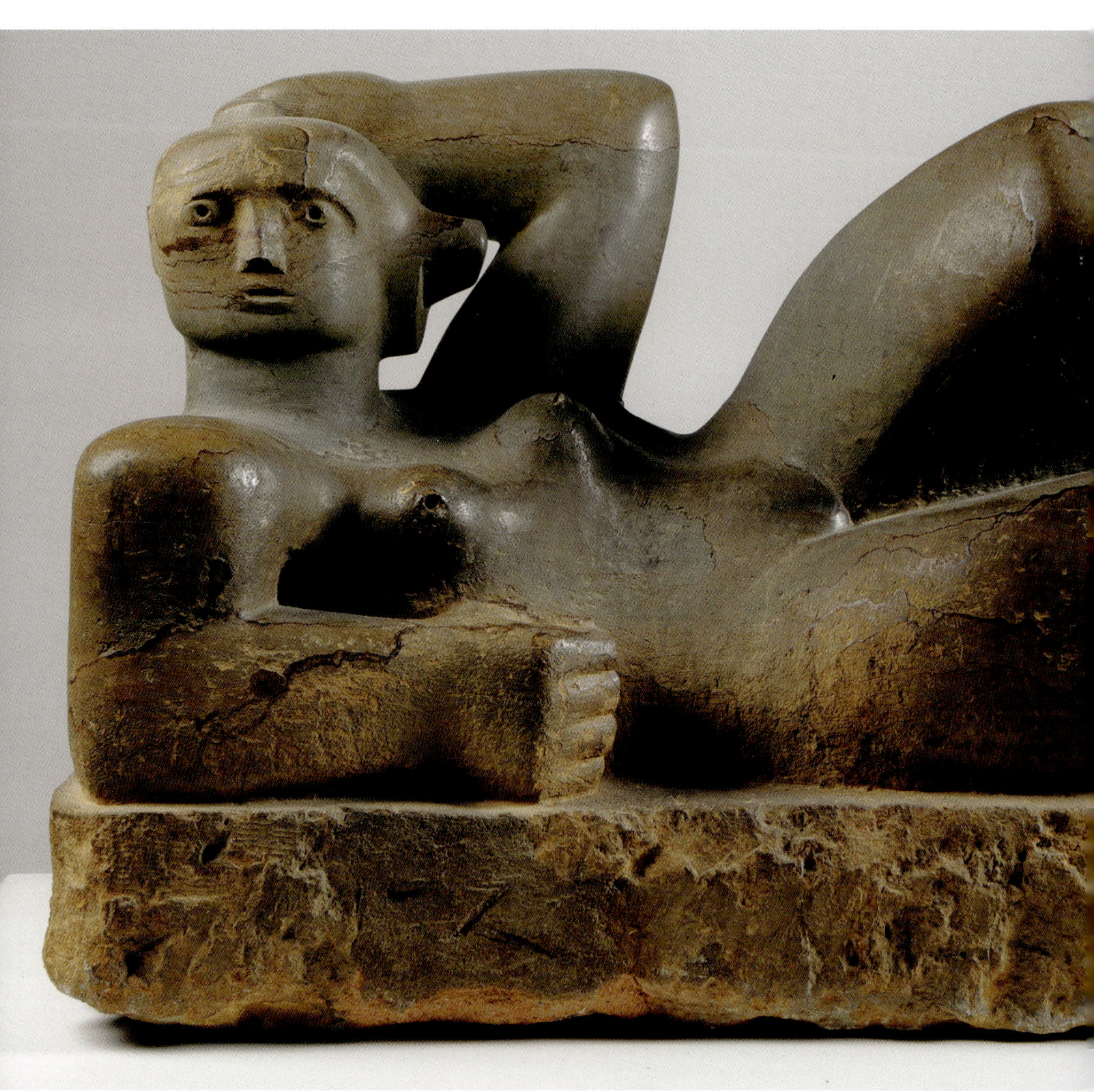

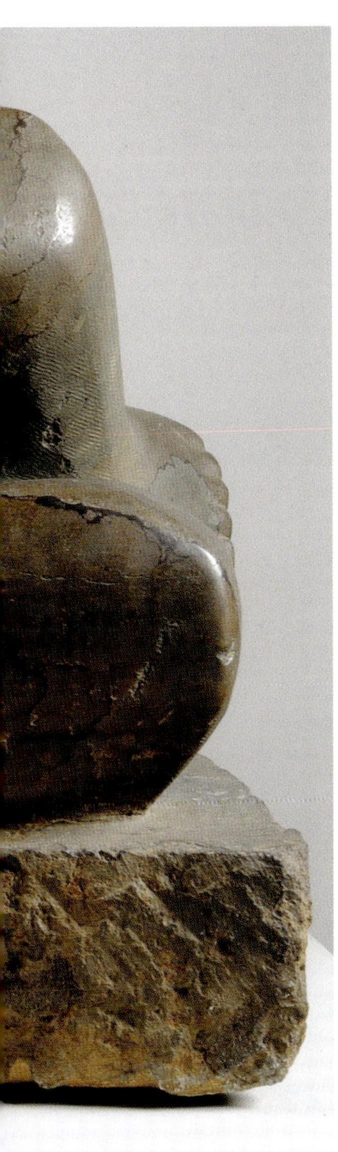

Reclining figure, 1929

Henry Moore, 1898–1986

Brown Hornton Stone, 54 × 82 × 37 cm

Purchased from the artist, 1941

LEEAG.SC.1941.10

No selection of works from Leeds would be complete without a Henry Moore sculpture. A Leeds alumnus and born locally in Castleford, there are few artists who have had the influence of Moore. Leeds Art Gallery is, of course, recognisable from the presence of his sculpture *Reclining Woman: Elbow* on the gallery steps; Moore himself laid the foundation stone and positioned the sculpture when the gallery was extended in 1982.

A major influence on our sculpture collection since 1982 has been The Henry Moore Foundation, which established the Henry Moore Institute in 1993. The institute manages the sculpture collection and archive on our behalf and through attracting leading scholars, curating displays and publishing research, has established Leeds as an international centre for the study and appreciation of sculpture.

This work is one of Moore's earliest sculptural achievements. It shows the essential ingredients of his practice, including his passion for the principle of 'truth to materials', his diverse range of artistic influences and the special relationship between the human figure and the landscape. Carved in Brown Hornton Stone, its simplified forms show the influence of Mexican sculpture, which Moore had discovered in the British Museum. The 'bumps and hollows' of the figure and the markings of the stone recall the undulations of a natural landscape. Moore himself reflected on this work as one of 'a list of ten or twenty works which I know have been key works and which I know have solved some directions that I wanted to be satisfied with… This had a freedom and yet kept a stormy strength and I knew when I finished it that it was the best sculpture I had done up to then.'

Praxitella, 1921

Percy Wyndham Lewis, 1882–1957

Oil on canvas, 141.2 × 101.6 cm

Gift from Edward Wadsworth through the Contemporary Art Society, 1945

LEEAG.PA.1945.15.1

This striking portrait is one of Leeds Art Gallery's best-known pictures. Wyndham Lewis, a founding but then defecting member of the Camden Town Group, was an influential figure. His art and writing was a celebration of the machine age and kicked against, or 'blasted', traditional Edwardian and Victorian culture. Before the war he developed his distinctive geometric abstract style, dubbed Vorticism, and he was the editor of 'BLAST', the short-lived magazine of the Vorticist movement.

During the First World War, Lewis served in the Royal Artillery on the Western front and was deeply affected by his experiences, writing vividly of artillery exchanges and several near-misses. On his return from service he took his art in a new direction. He introduced a satirical edge, painting a series of caricatures which he named 'Tyros', intended to comment on the 'new epoch' after the war. *Praxitella* is one of this series, a portrait of his then lover Iris Barry. It is characteristic of Lewis's postwar style in its impassiveness, the protective armour of the sitter shielding her emotions, giving her an inscrutable appearance. This is perhaps a reflection of the commonly held belief that all possible emotion had been expended during the war.

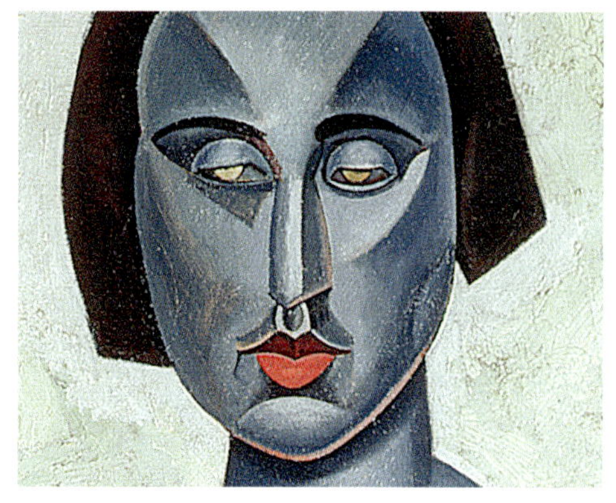

The work was given to Leeds in 1945 by the artist Edward Wadsworth through the Contemporary Art Society. The CAS has recently celebrated its centenary and is still helping galleries like ours acquire contemporary works of art either by gift or commission. Most recently we received funding for the 'Starting Point' programme which offered the opportunity for an emerging curator to work with our collections, and we were fortunate to be selected to receive a new work by artist DJ Simpson, *Common Field*.

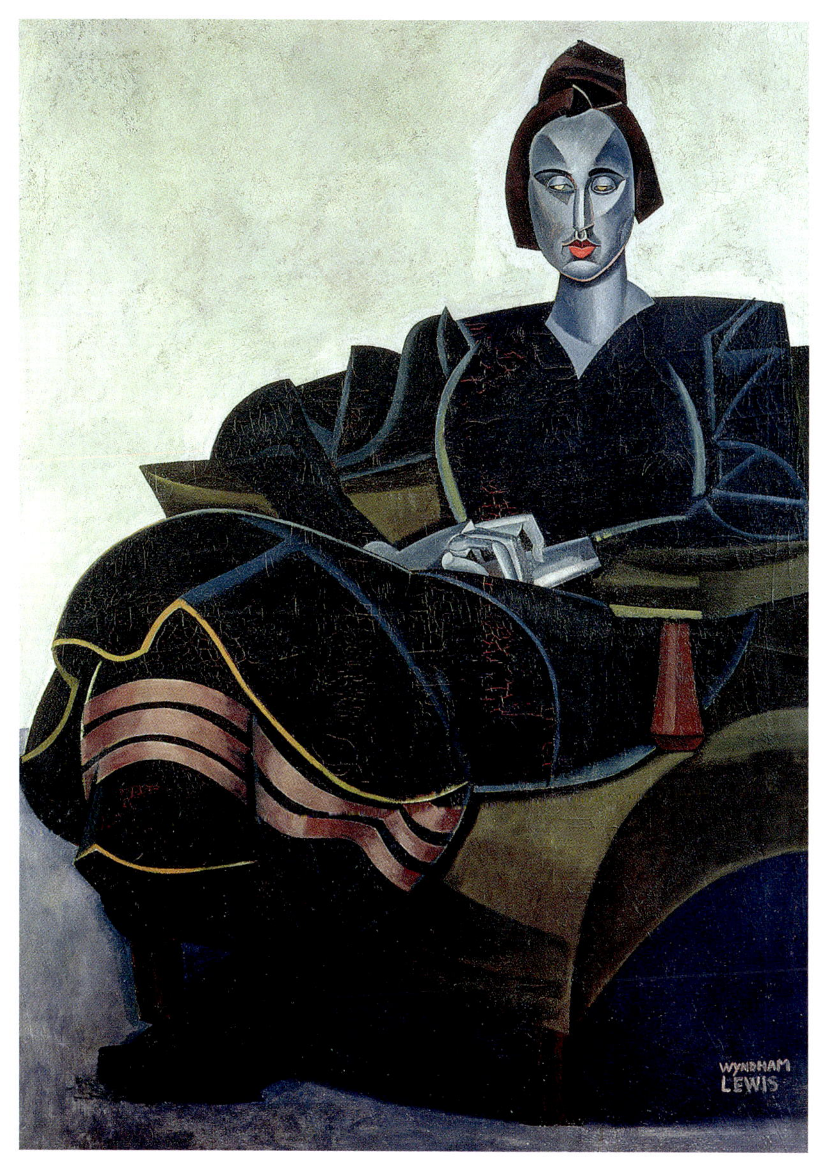
WYNDHAM
LEWIS

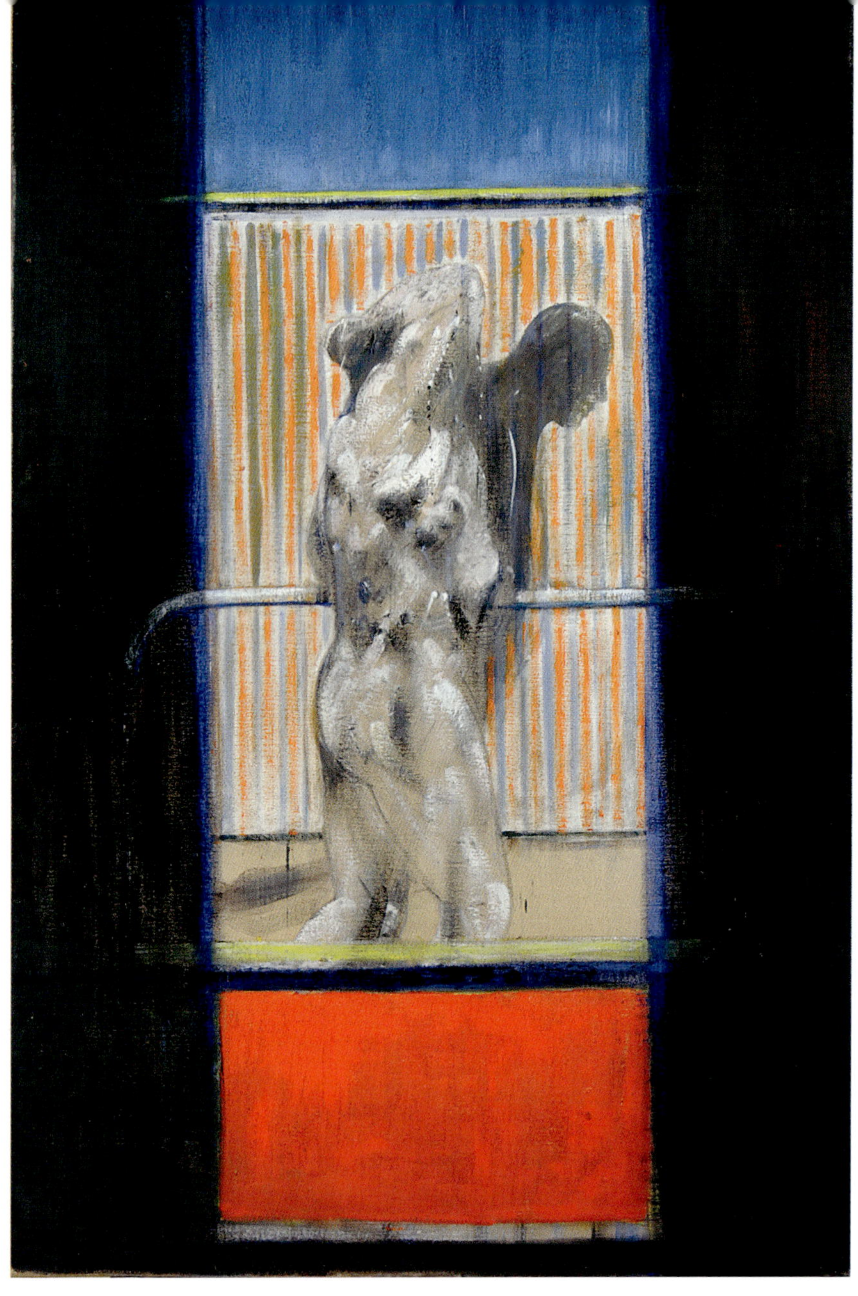

Painting, 1950

FRANCIS BACON, 1909–1992

Oil on canvas, 198.1 × 132.1 cm

Purchased by Leeds Art Fund, 1951

LEEAG.1951.15.LACF

THIS POWERFUL WORK by Francis Bacon was a controversial acquisition in 1951. Displayed in an exhibition of contemporary art in 1950 in Leeds Art Gallery, it captivated the Director, Ernest Musgrave, who vowed to secure it for the Leeds collections through the Leeds Art Fund (LAF).

With echoes of many visual sources reverberating in Bacon's imagination, including Eadweard Muybridge's photographs, Sickert and Michelangelo, this work has a terrific emotional intensity. Set against the backdrop of the postwar optimism of the Festival of Britain, it casts a menacing shadow. It was a picture that divided opinion: Musgrave was determined, writing, 'It reflects the artist's conception of the state of the world, the tension, secretive and latent violence of which we are all conscious.' He fought a campaign with the LAF to buy the work for £220, but there were many detractors, one saying, 'Bad draughtsmanship, crude colouring and deliberate ugliness cannot be excused because the painter has a headache about current events.' It was eventually put to a vote and it narrowly passed, securing the first Bacon for a regional gallery.

The LAF, one of the longest established friends organisations for the visual arts in the UK, was founded in 1912 by the Vice Chancellor of Leeds University, Michael Sadler, and Leeds Gallery curator, Frank Rutter. Over the century of its existence the organisation has supported the acquisition of in excess of 400 works for the collections in Leeds, and their valued support continues today. A membership comprising art enthusiasts and academics have over the years offered the galleries a keen eye, identifying works often from contemporary artists which have withstood the test of time.

Present party for you, 2012

Fiona Rae, 1963–

Oil and acrylic paint on canvas, 213.4 × 175.3 cm

Gift from Denise Coates and Richard Smith, 2012

LEEAG.2012.108

Fiona Rae's painting is one of the very latest to enter the collection. It is included here, not only as a startling example of contemporary abstract painting and as a declaration that painting is still very much alive today, but because it demonstrates a continuity of collecting. When Fiona Rae first exhibited at Leeds Art Gallery in 1990, in the British Art Show, she was part of a rebellious cohort of young artists that came to be known as the Young British Artists; she's now Professor of Painting at the Royal Academy Schools.

Rae has developed a distinctive language based on her own invention and imagination. Here, poured paint and brushed elements are held in sublime tension with Japanese animé, graphic design and kitsch imagery, all floating over a green background (never the most comfortable ground for an abstract painting). It is a picture of great energy and complexity, and not without humour: abstract painting for those who are perplexed by abstraction perhaps.

When we were putting together a funding strategy to buy this painting, after Leeds Art Gallery had organised an acclaimed new exhibition of Rae's work in 2012, her dealer gallery suggested one of the artist's long-standing patrons might be inclined to help by making a contribution. But they didn't want to; they chose instead to buy the painting outright and presented it to us as a gift. The Leeds collection has been built from such acts of private munificence, as well as the public purse, and it is heartening to know that the great benefactors of the past are echoed in such acts of philanthropy today.

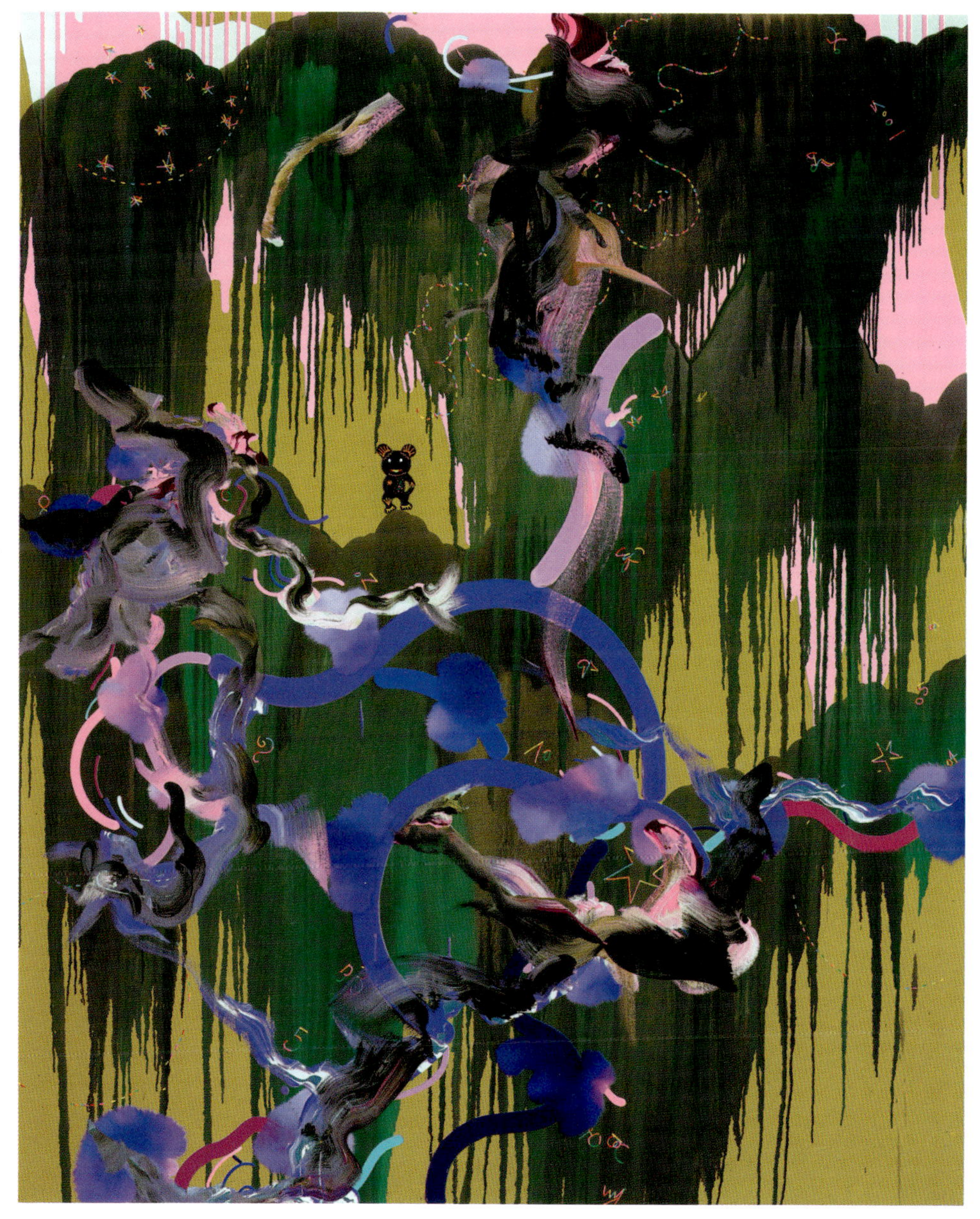

Dead Kingfisher, *c.*1816

JOSEPH MALLORD WILLIAM TURNER, 1775–1851

Watercolour on paper, 17.7 × 16.3 cm

Purchased at Sotheby's auction, 1985

LEEAG.1985.1q

J.M.W. TURNER, England's greatest landscape painter, is less well known for his more intimate sketches. This is one of 20 watercolours of birds that Leeds was able to save from export in 1985, when the Farnley estate near Otley was raising funds to restore the house. One of Turner's most important patrons was Farnley Hall's Walter Fawkes, who entertained Turner between 1808 and 1824. It was from Farnley that Turner explored Yorkshire and the north of England, creating sketches and watercolours, many of which are represented in the Leeds collections.

Turner produced these sketches whilst relaxing with friends out hunting on the Farnley estate. They were compiled for a five-volume *Ornithological Collection* series of albums for Fawkes's library. The collection of albums covers birds from across Britain and details features and points of interest to the keen ornithologist. The sketches, of mainly Yorkshire species, many of them game birds, were accompanied by sections cut from Thomas Bewick's *History of British Birds* and served as a unique reference for Fawkes's interest. It is notable too that Turner shared this interest in ornithology, and looking again at many of Turner's works you will often see a bird somewhere.

The kingfisher stands out as it demonstrates Turner's perfect grasp of colour. Even though the bird is lying dead, there is a vibrancy to the plumage, and the reflectivity of the feathers is rendered beautifully. In life, a kingfisher on the wing is the merest flash of metallic blue and orange, so different from the mottled browns of most British birds, and it is clear that Turner wished to capture this vividness.

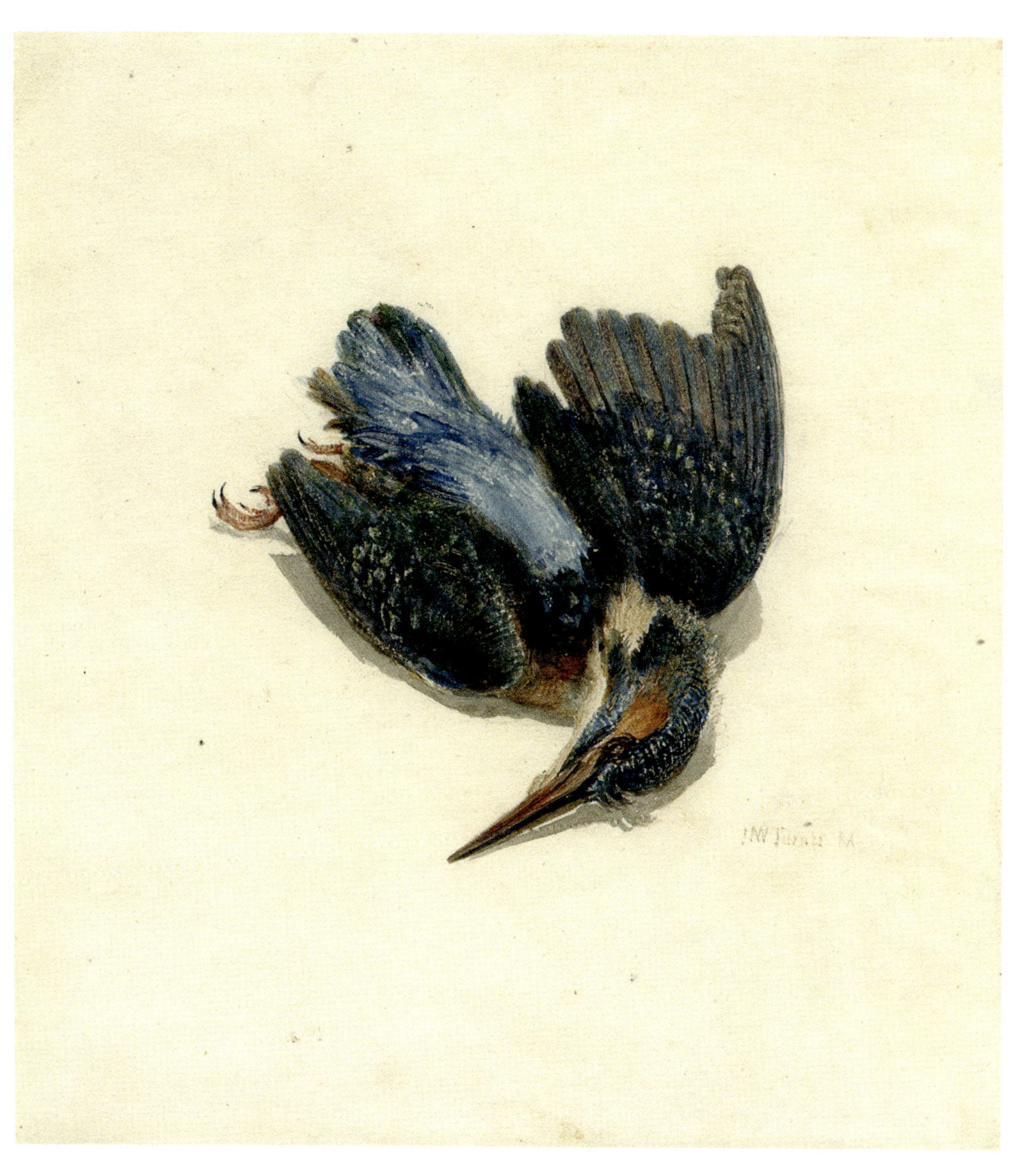

View of Kirkstall Abbey, 1860

George A. Fripp, 1813–1896
Watercolour on paper, 52.5 × 86 cm
Gift from Sir Edward Brotherton, 1926
LEEAG.1926.669

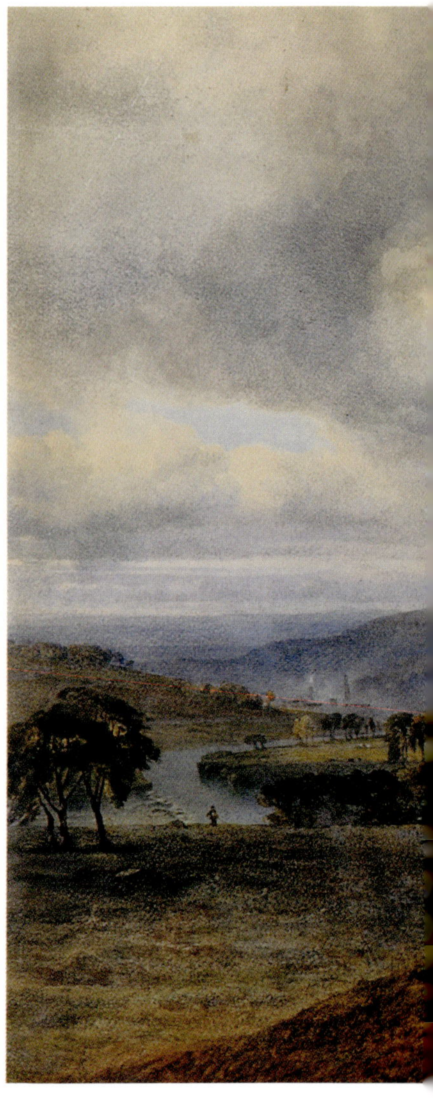

Local topography is well represented in our acclaimed collection of works on paper, the Yorkshire landscape being a compelling subject for any artist. And standing tall on the banks of the river Aire, Kirkstall Abbey has been a subject for generations of painters. Turner, Cotman and Girtin all studied the abbey through drawings and watercolours, and many of the results are held in our collections. I have selected this charming depiction of the abbey by the distinguished though little-known Victorian watercolour painter, George Fripp.

Founded in 1152, Kirkstall Abbey was built by Henry de Lacy, who vowed to dedicate an abbey to the Virgin Mary should he survive a serious illness; he did, and kept his promise. Built as a daughter abbey to Fountains Abbey, it was a working monastery up until the dissolution of the monasteries. It is one of the most complete examples of a Cistercian abbey in Britain, retaining a great deal of the abbey complex, including the original gatehouse, now Abbey House Museum.

Viewed from the east, the abbey, illuminated by bright sunshine, looms above the rural landscape. And yet encroaching from the west are the signs of industry – for to the left of the abbey, under a cloud and through the haze of smog, is Kirkstall forge. There had been a forge in the same location since the thirteenth century but in 1860 the productivity of the forge was increasing under the momentum of the Industrial Revolution, as was the case all over Leeds. Fripp's sense of foreboding is made plain – that the dark clouds of heavy industry would change this idyllic northern landscape forever.

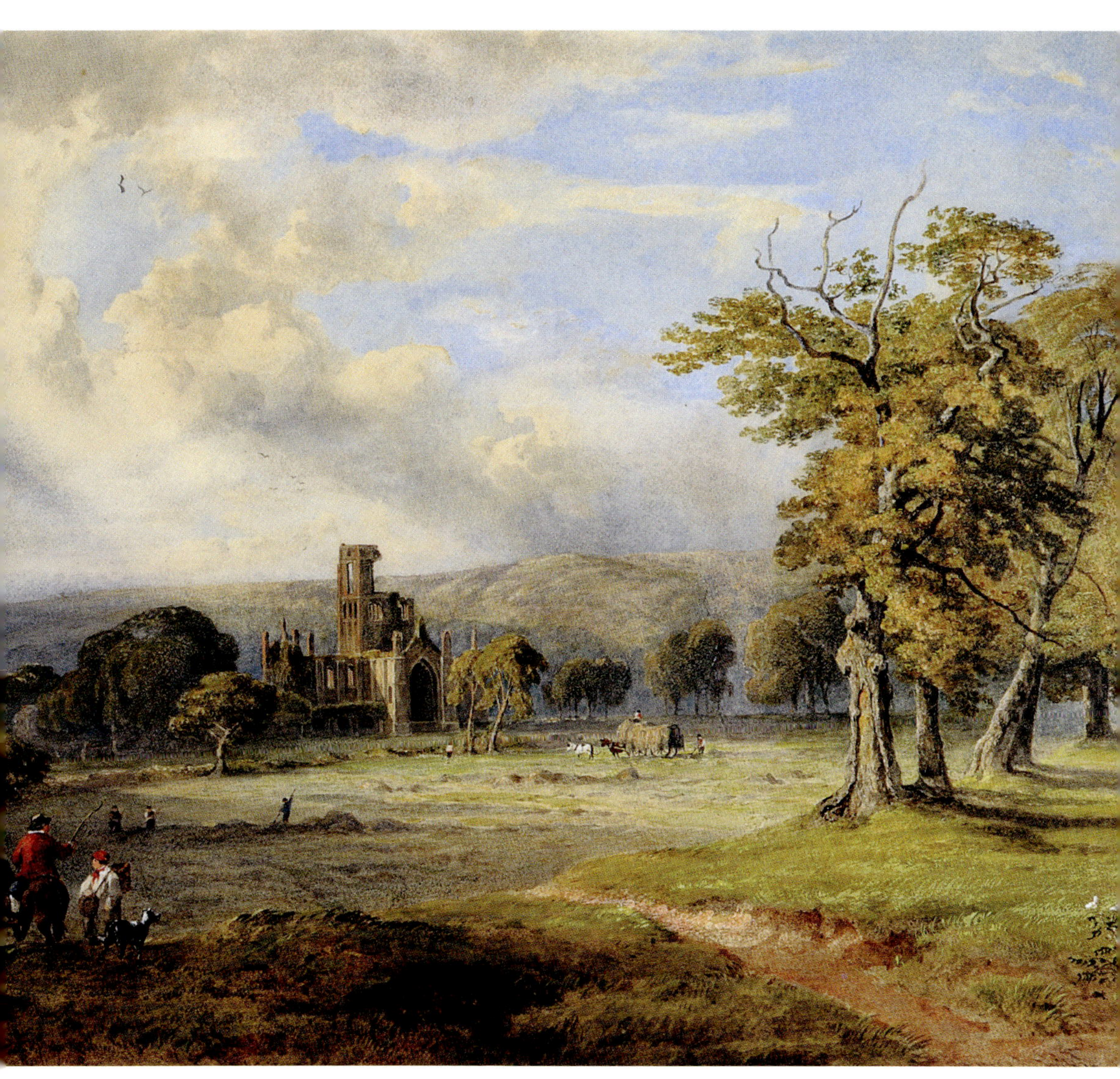

Irish House of Commons, 1780

Francis Wheatley, 1747–1801
Oil on canvas, 172.5 × 215.9 cm
Gift from Gascoigne, 1968
LEEAG.1968.7.22

This commanding painting hangs in the elegant dining room of Lotherton Hall, former home of the Gascoigne family, which was given to the city in 1968 by Sir Alvary Gascoigne and his wife. Whilst there are no definitive records of when this picture was bought, it first appeared on an inventory in 1843. This was just after the death of Richard Oliver Gascoigne, so we suspect it was he who acquired it for Parlington Hall, a former seat of the family. This painting puts into context the complex nature of Anglo-Irish relations of the time. Richard Oliver came from an Anglo-Irish Protestant family. He was the stepson-in-law of Sir Thomas Gascoigne, 8th and last baronet of Parlington. Sir Thomas named him his heir on condition that he assumed the Gascoigne name and arms.

The picture portrays the famous parliamentary occasion in 1780 when Henry Grattan proposed the repeal of Poyning's Law, which severely limited Ireland's control of its own affairs. Shortly after this debate the chamber burned down and this is the only surviving record of it in use. The detail is extraordinary – each member has his portrait faithfully executed and almost all are identifiable. A key published in 1801 omits to indicate who was in the gallery where the ladies can be seen – women were not permitted entry so it is likely that those depicted paid to be included in the painted scene.

The artist was Francis Wheatley, a highly talented yet rather reckless character who was admitted to the Royal Academy in 1791. During the period when he fled his debtors, and an irate cuckolded husband in London for Dublin (with the wife of said husband), he painted what are arguably his most accomplished works, of which this is his masterpiece.

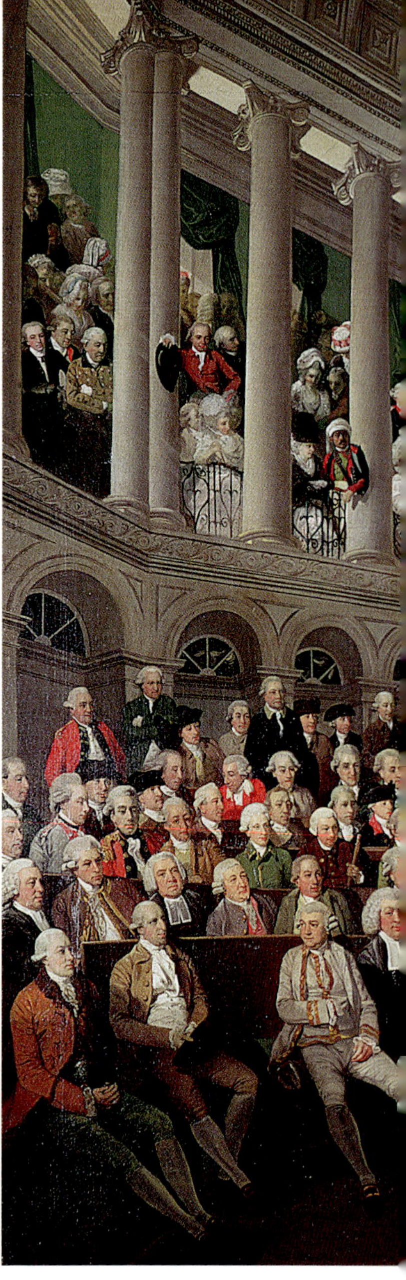

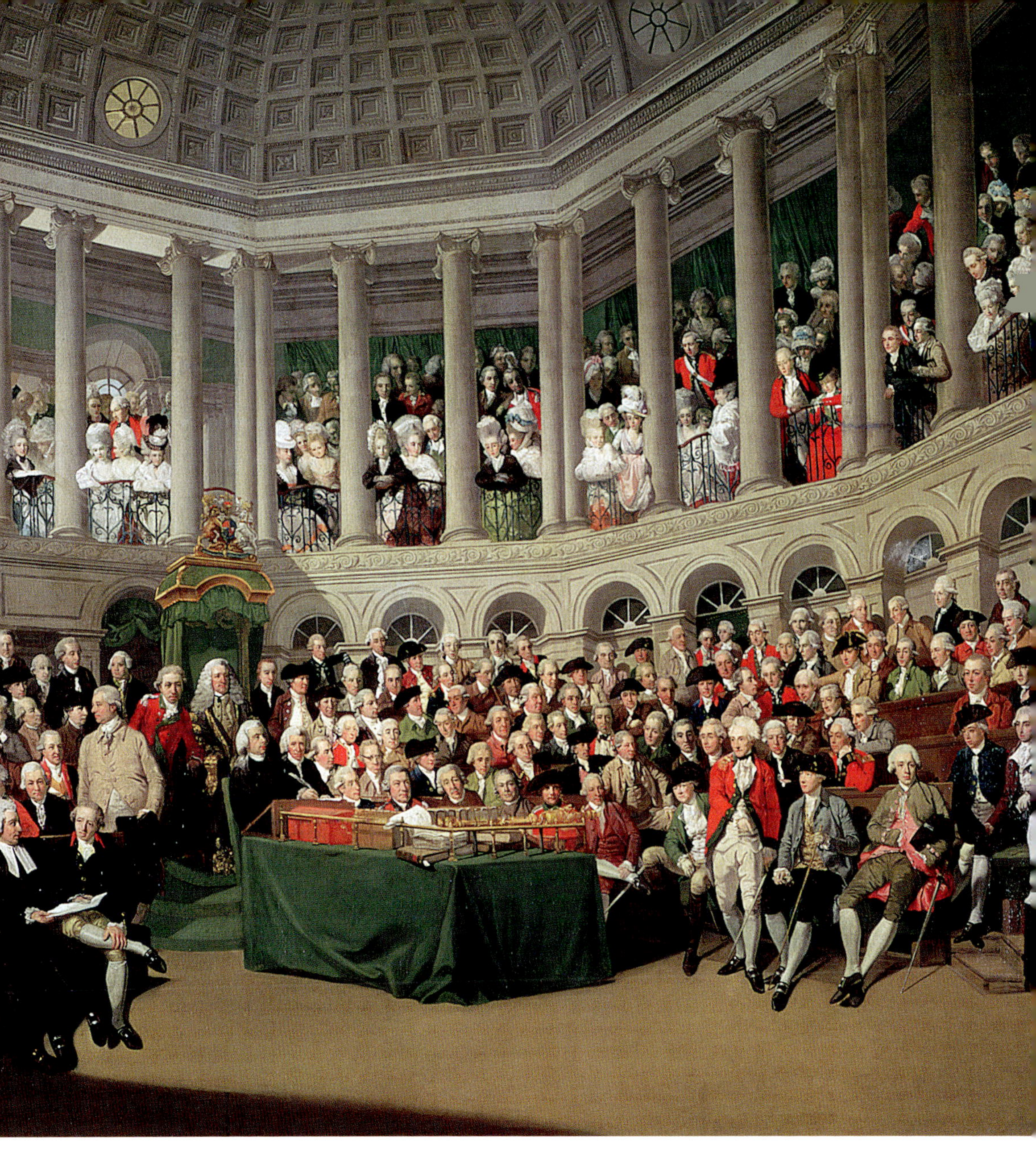

Park Row, Leeds, 1882

John Atkinson Grimshaw, 1836–1893
Oil on canvas, 76.2 × 63.5 cm
Purchased at Sotheby's auction, 1987
LEEAG.1987.19

John Atkinson Grimshaw is one of the best-known Leeds artists of the second half of the nineteenth century. Like his contemporary, the landscape artist J.W. Inchbold, Grimshaw was influenced by the style, technique and colour of the Pre-Raphaelites in his early works in the 1860s. However, by 1870 Grimshaw had evolved his signature style, focusing on nocturnal scenes, often depicting the docks or river views of Liverpool, Leeds and London. He also painted suburban scenes – of lanes lit by moonlight shining through branches onto wet cobbled streets lined with stone walls behind which lay mysterious mansions. Grimshaw is appreciated today for the poetic and nostalgic mood conveyed in his Victorian scenes, a reminder of city life 140 years ago.

This scene of Park Row in Leeds was commissioned by the directors of Beckett's Bank to record Gilbert Scott's splendid gothic building, seen to the right. On the left is the portico of the Philosophical Hall, the museum of the Leeds Philosophical and Literary Society and the original Leeds City Museum. Park Row, described at the time as the Pall Mall of Leeds, was one of the main commercial thoroughfares of the new city. Its large imposing buildings exuded confidence and an exuberance that characterised the growing city.

Alas, several of the buildings in this scene have been demolished – the museum was damaged by a bomb in the Second World War and eventually pulled down in 1965; and St Anne's Roman Catholic Cathedral, seen at the far end, was demolished in 1901.

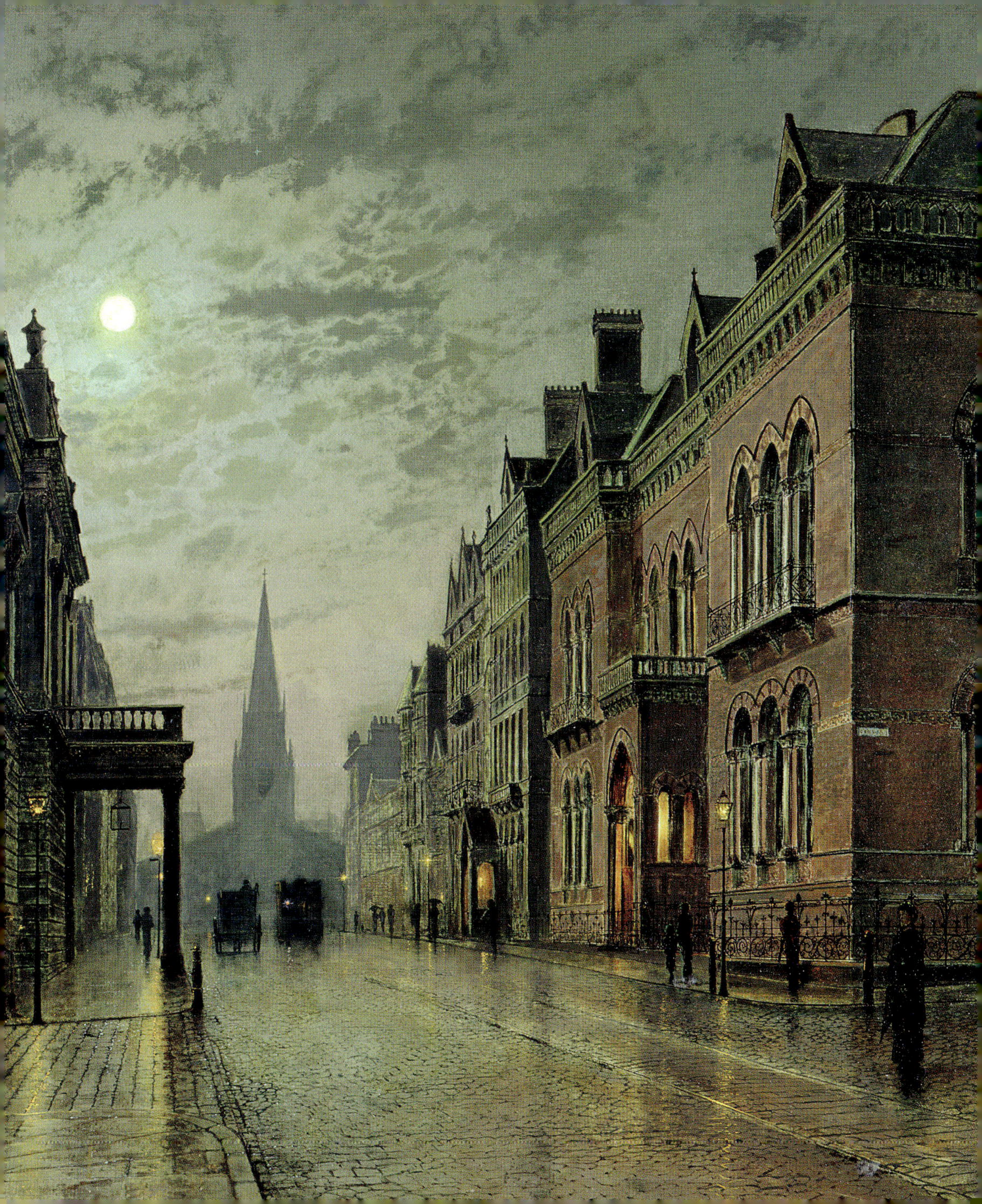

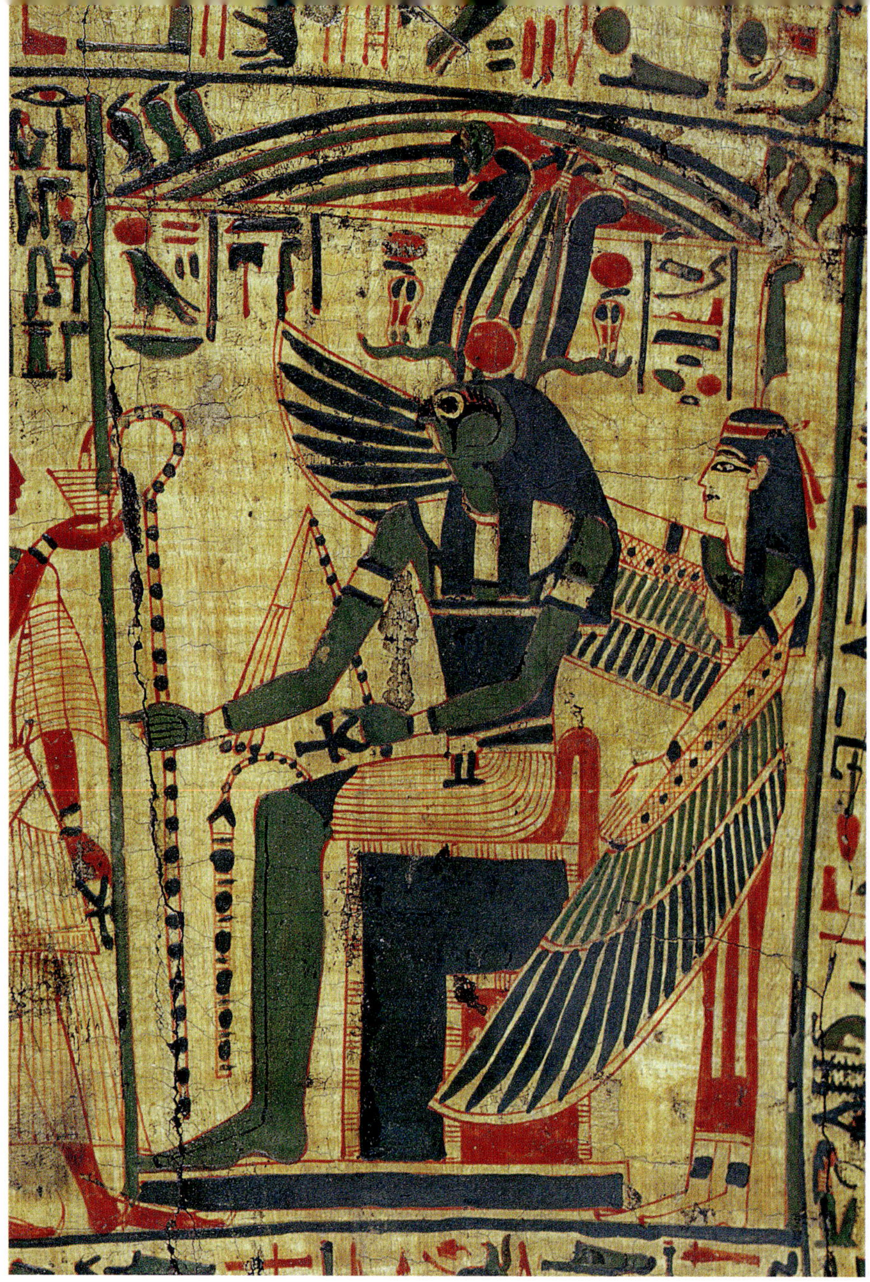

Coffin of Nesyamun, *c.*1100 BC

Egypt, New Kingdom, 20th dynasty

Wood, gypsum plaster, paint, 195 × 59 × 30 cm

Gift from John Blayds, 1823

LEEDM.D.1960.426.3

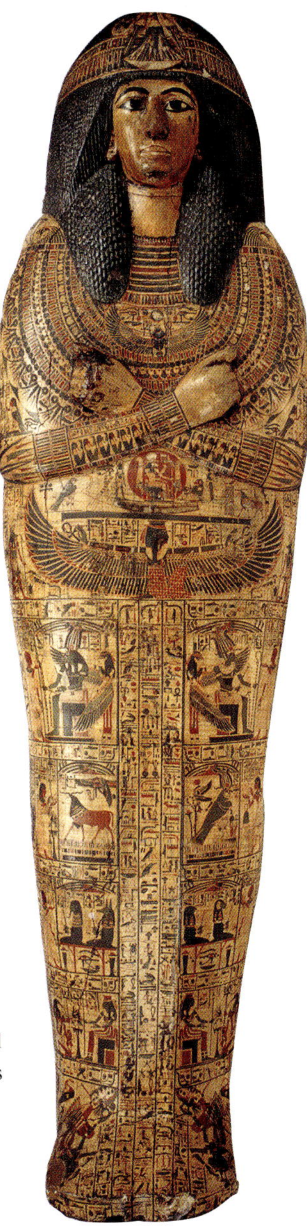

THE COLLECTIONS OF Leeds City Museum (and Discovery Centre) date back to 1819 to the establishment of the Leeds Philosophical and Literary Society (LPLS). Founded to 'discuss all the branches of Natural Knowledge and Literature, but excluding all topics of Religion, Politics and Ethics', it was to be at the forefront of the city's intellectual life. The Society amassed collections of natural history, anthropology and antiquities for its museum on Park Row. These were transferred to the city in 1921 and whilst the original building has gone, the two new premises, I hope, are a fitting legacy.

One of our most famous exhibits in the City Museum is Nesyamun – The Leeds Mummy. We know from a leather ornament in his bandages that he died in the reign of Ramesses XI, 1113–1085 BC. The evidence suggests Nesyamun was a high-ranking priest, incense-bearer and scribe at the temple of Amun in the Karnak complex at Thebes. Known as a 'waab priest', he had attained a high level of purification and was therefore permitted to approach the statue of Amun in the sacred inner sanctum of the temple.

The outer coffin is painted with scenes from the Book of the Dead and show Nesyamun making offerings to various deities. The texts, written by a single author in Middle Egyptian, contain prayers to the gods and goddesses asking for success in the afterlife and contact with the gods. The mummy was the subject of the first multidisciplinary mummy investigation and has remained the focus of much analysis ever since, including a forensic facial reconstruction. Recent studies have investigated Nesyamun's life and the cause of his death – a pathological analysis suggests a severe allergic reaction may have brought about his demise.

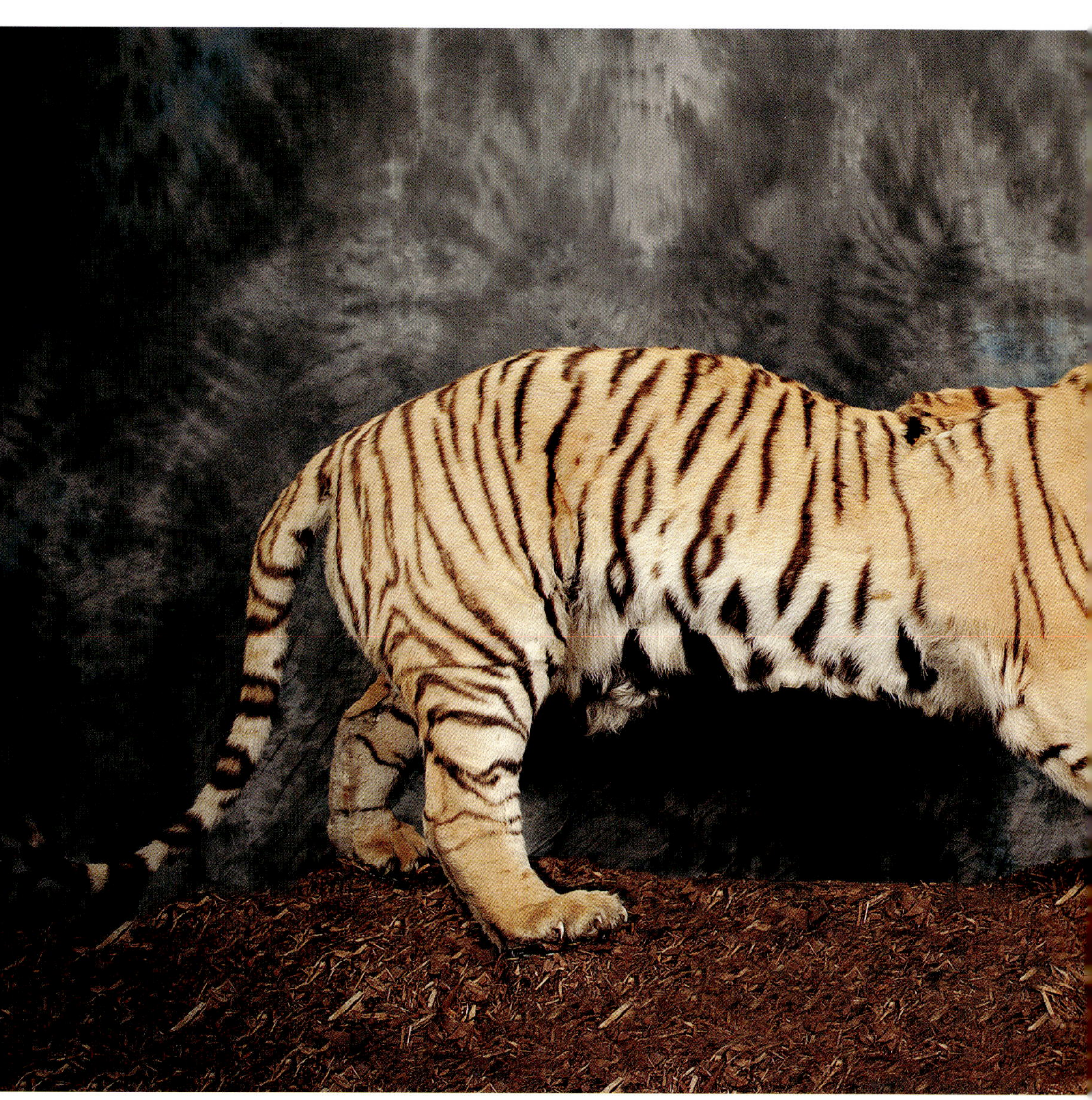

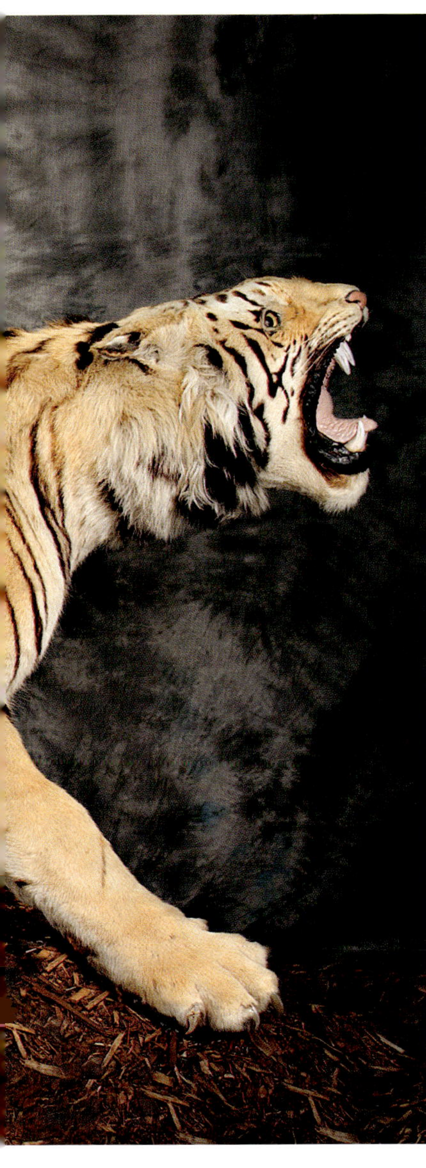

***Bengal tiger*, 1860**

HENRY WARD (taxidermist), London

Mount, 140 × 260 × 100 cm

Presented by William Gott, 1862

LEEDM.C.1862.29.13

ONE OF THE MOST ICONIC specimens in the Leeds collections, and certainly the most recognisable, is the Leeds Tiger. It is the centrepiece of the City Museum, loved by generations of visitors and probably the most photographed of all our objects.

The tiger was shot by Major-General Sir Charles Reid at Dehra Dun in the Himalayas in March 1860, apparently because it had become a nuisance to a nearby village. Reid was a highly decorated soldier, having commanded the Sirmoor Battalion during the Indian rebellion of 1857. He was credited with firing the first shots on the rebels and executing the first mutineers following the uprising in Meerut in May of that same year.

Once shot, the pelt was prepared as a rug and shipped to the UK as an impressive trophy. After display in the Indian court of the London International Exhibition in 1862, the skin was purchased by William Gott, who had it mounted by taxidermist Henry Ward for presentation to the LPLS. We suspect that the pelt was combined with other tiger skins, and the stuffing is straw. These factors, along with the distortions caused by it having been initially prepared as a rug, contribute to the rather unusual shape and great size of the mount.

After mounting it was pronounced to be 'unequalled in Europe, either for its extraordinary size or its artistic and life-like setting up'. Reports of the time describe its popularity: 'It has been fitly placed in the centre of the large Zoological Room, and is always the most attractive object in that collection.' This is still true today, as he guards the entrance to our *Life on Earth* gallery.

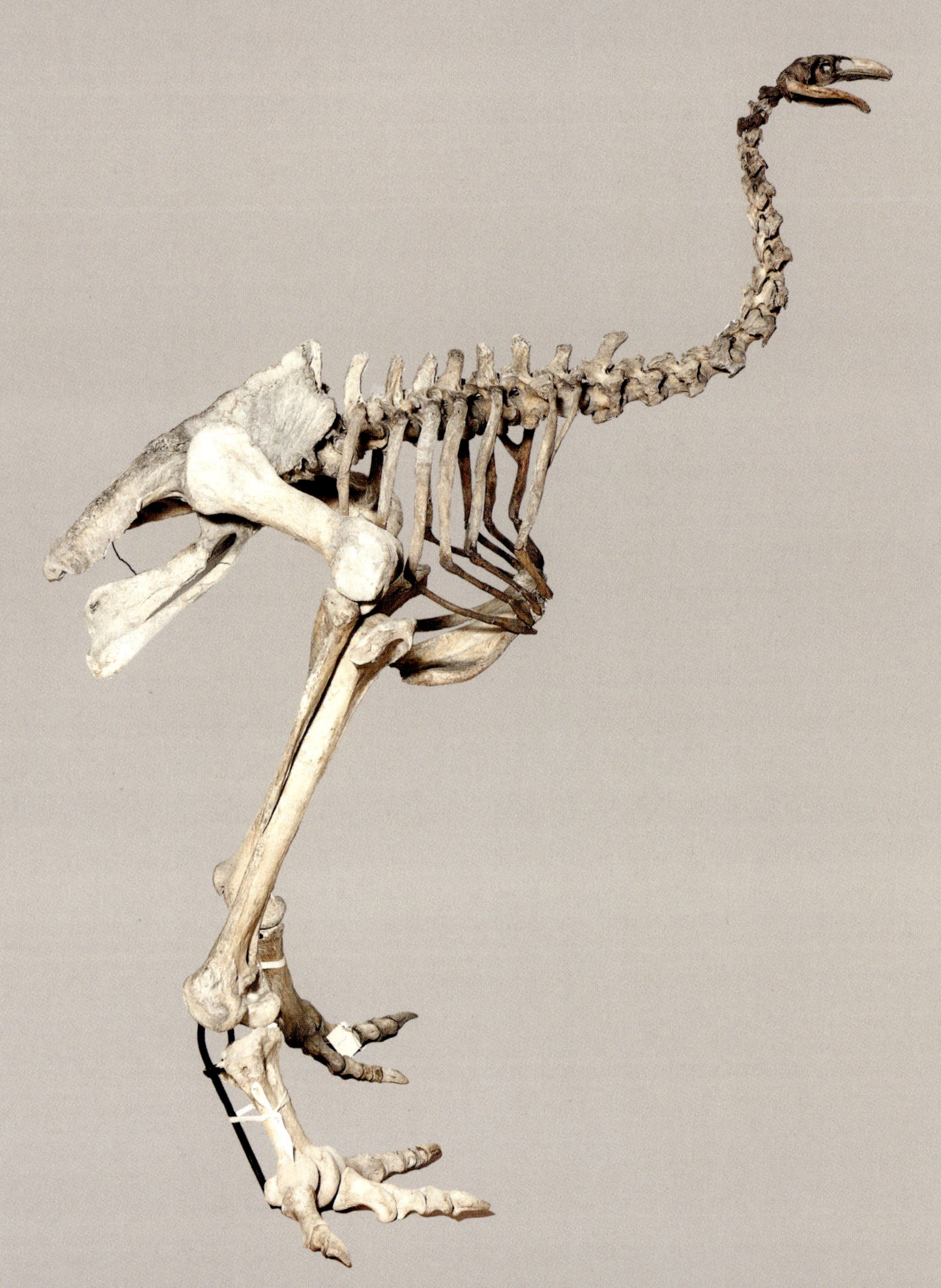

Heavy-footed moa, 1868

Assembled by NIGEL LARKIN, 2011

Bone, steel, cherry wood, 139 × 84 × 117 cm

Purchased by subscription, 1868

LEEDM.C.1868.6

THE LEEDS NATURAL HISTORY collections are particularly strong in exotic species. From the outset the LPLS collected native and exotic material both from the field and through donation and purchase. We have an enviable range of large exotic animals and in particular extinct and endangered species. Amongst the Tasmanian wolves, dodo, giant deer, great auk and passenger pigeons is this rather impressive skeletal mount of a heavy-footed moa, an extinct flightless bird from New Zealand.

The skeleton was purchased for the collections by the LPLS. Presumably due to the cost, it was bought by subscription by Dr Charles Chadwick, Messrs J.G. Marshall, Arthur Marshall, S.J. Brown, Thomas Harvey and Miss H. Dawson. That local people were persuaded to subscribe to the purchase of such an important specimen reflects the confidence the city had in its scientific standing, but also how such specimens were used as status symbols. The specimen is remarkable in itself but at the time it was the only example of this species in Britain, outside the British Museum in London. The skeleton, like many Victorian preparations, is a composite of more than one individual, as the London specimen was.

Natural history specimens with good data are always scientifically valuable, but extinct species are also extremely important, and museums are the last places where the remains of these animals are preserved and made available for research. We have a large amount of moa material but this particular skeleton is by far the most important piece in the collection given its excellent provenance and completeness. This moa was conserved and articulated in 2011 and I doubt it has ever looked better.

Gorilla 'Mok', 1938

E. Gerrard & Sons, taxidermists, 1930s

Mount, 154 × 121 × 94 cm

Purchased from E. Gerrard & Sons, 1938

LEEDM.C.1938.40.1.4079

This magnificent mount of a western lowland gorilla is affectionately named 'Mo Koundje' or simply 'Mok'. He is one of the most charismatic specimens in the collection, with a rather poignant story. He was born in French Equatorial Africa where he was trapped and taken to Paris. He was displayed for a short time in a cage in the lobby of a hotel before he was purchased by London Zoo in August 1932, along with a female gorilla, 'Moina'. The pair were exhibited in a purpose-built gorilla house from 1933 and they became quite the celebrities, often featuring in the national newspapers and the subject of much comment.

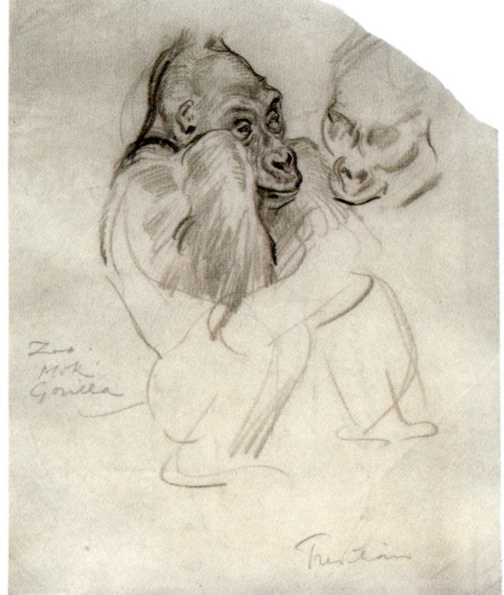

A pencil sketch of the time by Cecil Stuart Tresilian (shown right) captures a rather subdued-looking character in the zoo. Zoo-keeping at that time was not as well informed as it is today: Mok, a herbivore, was fed a diet of steak and chicken, which shortened his life. He died of kidney disease at London Zoo on 14 January 1938, aged just seven years. He was followed shortly afterwards by Moina, who became distracted after Mok died, picking at sores on her feet which became infected. Mok's death was big news in the press and the story caught the eye of the LPLS, who often acquired specimens from London Zoo. Mok's carcass was taken to a taxidermist, who prepared the mount we have today and the skeleton, also in our collection.

It is sobering to think that after a short life of captivity and exhibition Mok has spent the most part of the last 80 years in the public gaze, but I hope that as a museum specimen he is a powerful tool for enabling understanding of animal welfare and conservation.

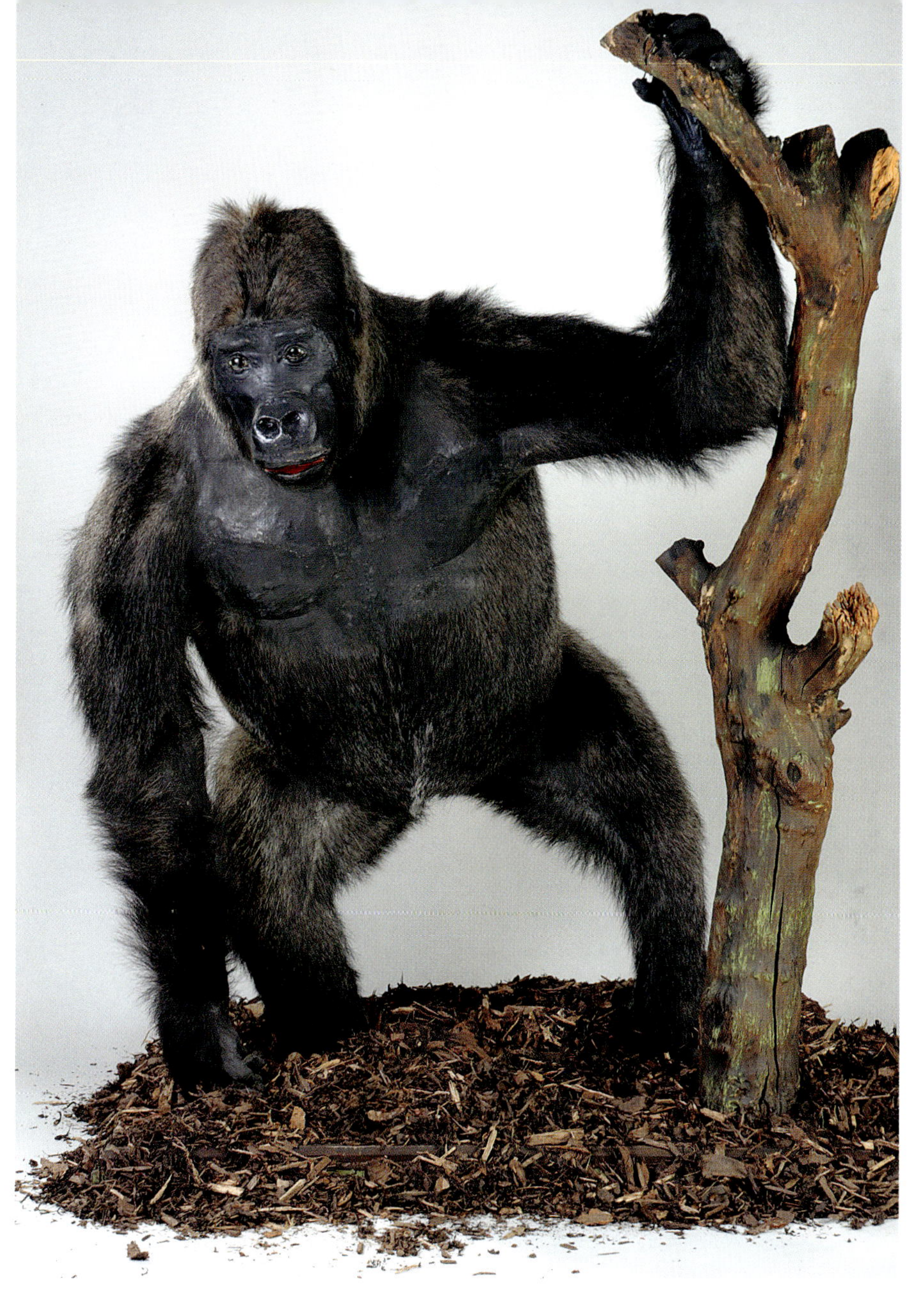

Bear skull, 600,000–11,500 YEARS BP

Ireland

Osteological preparation, 17 × 22 × 43 cm
Presented to Leeds Philosophical and Literary Society, 1864
LEEDM.B.1864.38.1

NATURAL HISTORY COLLECTIONS tend to be the largest in multidisciplinary museums; numerous, often unfathomable to the untrained eye and yet containing items you would run into a fire to save. Individual specimens of every known species of living organism are described and published in scientific literature according to precise international rules. Those specimens become the ultimate reference specimens against which all other examples are compared, and are designated the 'type specimen' of that species. Because they need to be easily retrieved for study, these specimens are held in museum collections, making museums essential repositories for science. Often they are historic, having been described during the boom in natural history in the nineteenth century, but species are often reclassified and new discoveries described. Leeds, like many other large regional collections, holds several such specimens.

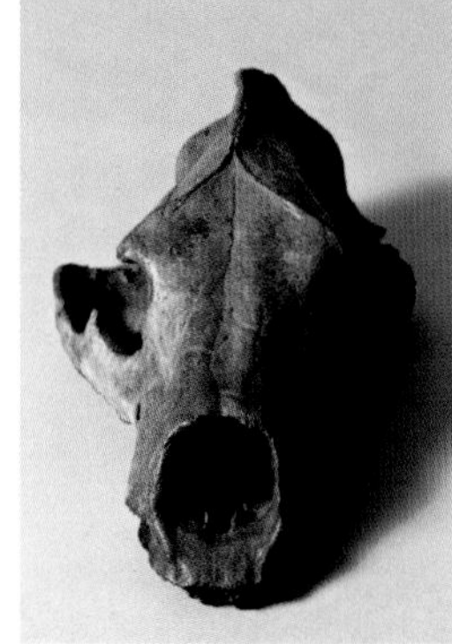

This large skull is the type specimen of the extinct bear, *Ursus Planafrons*. Excavated from a peat bog in Co. Westmeath, Ireland, it was given to the LPLS in 1864 and was studied by then curator Henry Denny. Although Denny's specialism was entomology, he famously corresponded with Darwin about lice, and he was an excellent all-round naturalist. He sent photographs of the skull to the famous Victorian anatomist Professor Owen, of the British Museum, who advised him that it was likely to be a new species. Denny published the description in 1864 and it was designated the type specimen.

The study of specimens like this for bear evolution continues today. Recent research has found evidence that all modern polar bears are descended from hybrids of ancient polar and brown bears, reflecting the changing climate during the Ice Age. Specimens such as this one are key evidence of this, showing how an old skull from a bog can provide up-to-the-minute scientific information for globally significant subjects such as climate change.

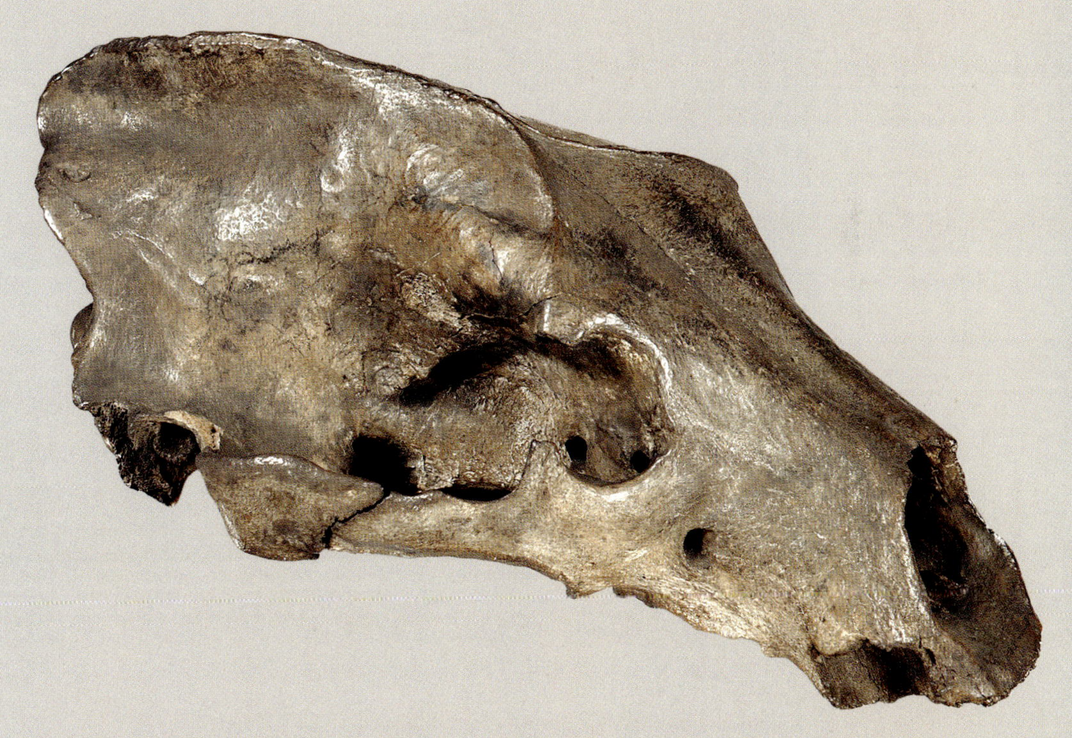

Schorl in smoky quartz, *c.*1804–19

Yekaterinburg, Russia

Quartz, schorl, 5.4 × 5.2 × 18.4 cm

Purchased, Sir Alexander Crichton collection, 1826

LEEDM.B.1826.23

Often in the shadow of the larger and more showy exhibits in a museum, minerals can be of considerable scientific and historic importance, as well as being quite beautiful. In fact, the stories of how minerals find their way into museum collections can rival those of any work of art.

This rather handsome specimen of a schorl (black tourmaline) crystal cutting through a large crystal of smoky quartz was collected from Yekaterinburg, Russia, by Sir Alexander Crichton, noted physician and mineral collector. As for many gentlemen of his time, natural history was a keen interest of his and as Crichton travelled across Europe studying medicine, he developed a connoisseur's eye for minerals. Over the course of 40 years he amassed a collection of over 4,000 specimens of the highest quality, acquired in large part from Russia and Siberia during his years in St Petersburg from 1803, when he was appointed personal physician to Tsar Alexander I of Russia. This was a highly successful career move

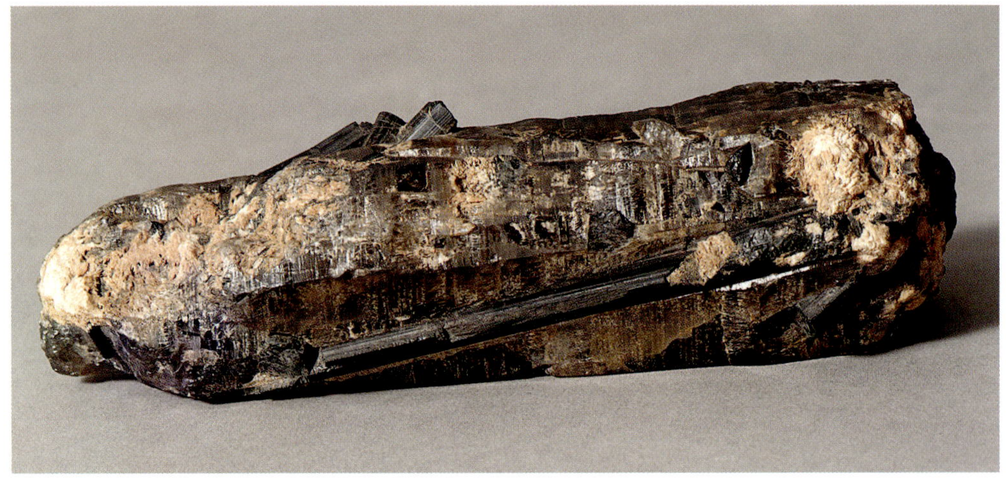

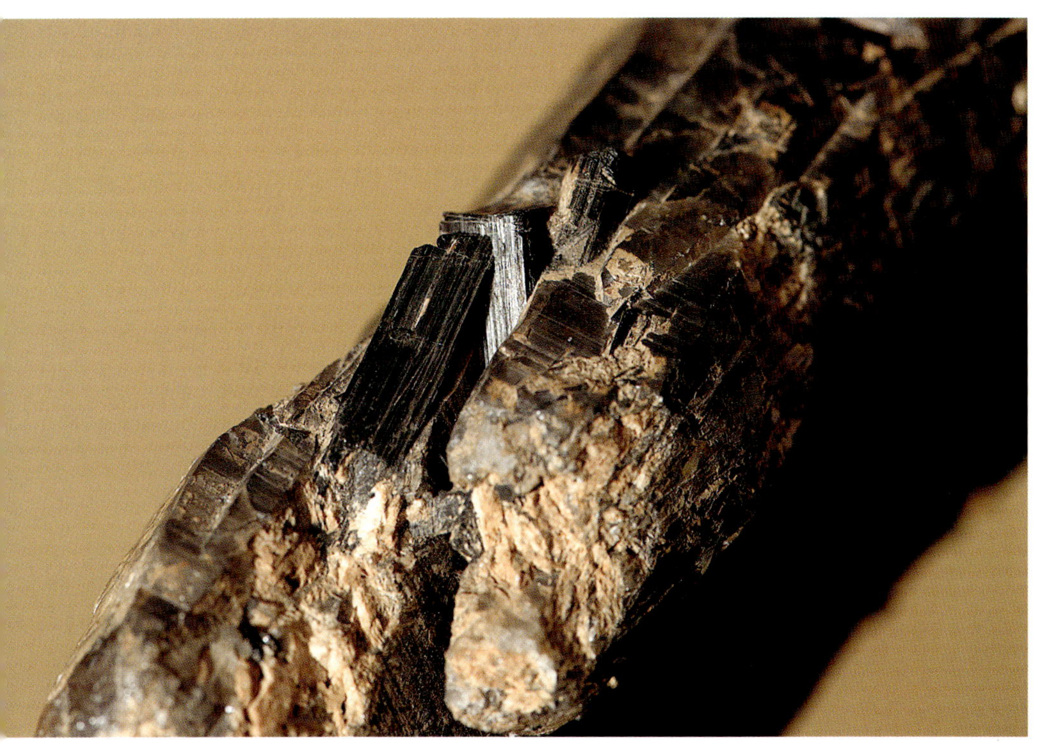

which meant he had the means to pursue his passion for mineral collecting. A friend said of his collection: 'Nothing is found therein which cannot make a claim to being extraordinary. All is chosen according to strict criteria, with the most refined taste and the finest delicacy...'

By 1826 Crichton had returned to England. Retired from medicine and withdrawing from public life, he commissioned the auction of his entire collection. The LPLS at this time was growing its collection at a significant rate and was collecting minerals beyond the geology of the 'neighbourhood of Leeds'. When the auction was announced, the Society recognised an opportunity but lack of funds precluded their making a grant; instead £84 was raised by subscription from 62 members, and 250 of the rarest and most beautiful specimens were purchased.

Painted ivory tusk, 1933

Jewish

Ivory, paint, copper, 137 × 10.7 cm
On loan from HM Revenue and Customs, 1983
LEEDM.F.L.1983.6.1A

In 2012 for the Cultural Olympiad we staged an exhibition called *Treasured: Smuggled? Stolen? Saved?* It was an exhibition entirely conceived, researched, designed and built by the team of young people involved with us who call themselves the Preservative Party. They were inspired by the stories of how items in the collection came to be in Leeds and it stimulated their interest to explore the issues and ethics around collecting. The discussions they had around matters such as import of cultural property, restitution and spoilation, and the ethics of human remains, were stimulating and thought-provoking, and the resulting exhibition was a triumph.

One item which particularly resonated was this elaborately painted elephant tusk, confiscated by HM Customs from a Jewish Iranian family fleeing the Islamic revolution in Iran in the early 1980s (the family had been unable to prove it was a family heirloom). Scenes on the tusk depict episodes from the life of Moses and other events recorded in the Torah (the Jewish equivalent of the Christian Old Testament). Shoshona Angyalfi, a Hebrew teacher, translated the inscriptions on the tusk, and a recording of her reading the inscriptions was available in the exhibition. A key inscription gives a place name, Isfahan, and a date, 5694 (equivalent to AD 1933). So whilst it appears to be an antique, the

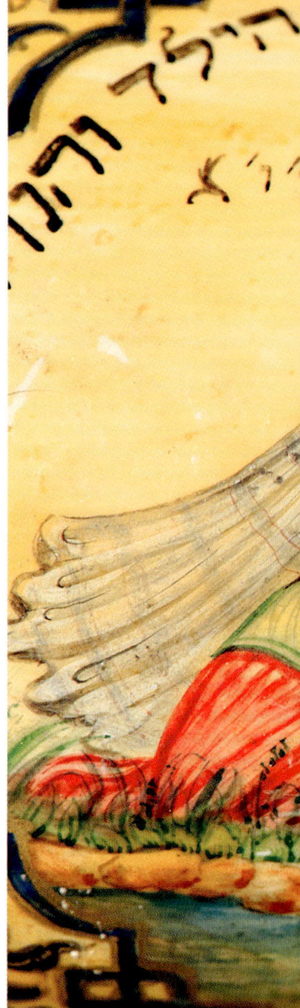

tusk is in fact a twentieth-century piece, albeit with an extraordinary history. We were offered the tusk on loan in 1983 to educate the public about the laws protecting endangered species from import and export. Maybe one day the family who had to leave it at Heathrow will learn how treasured this item is in Leeds.

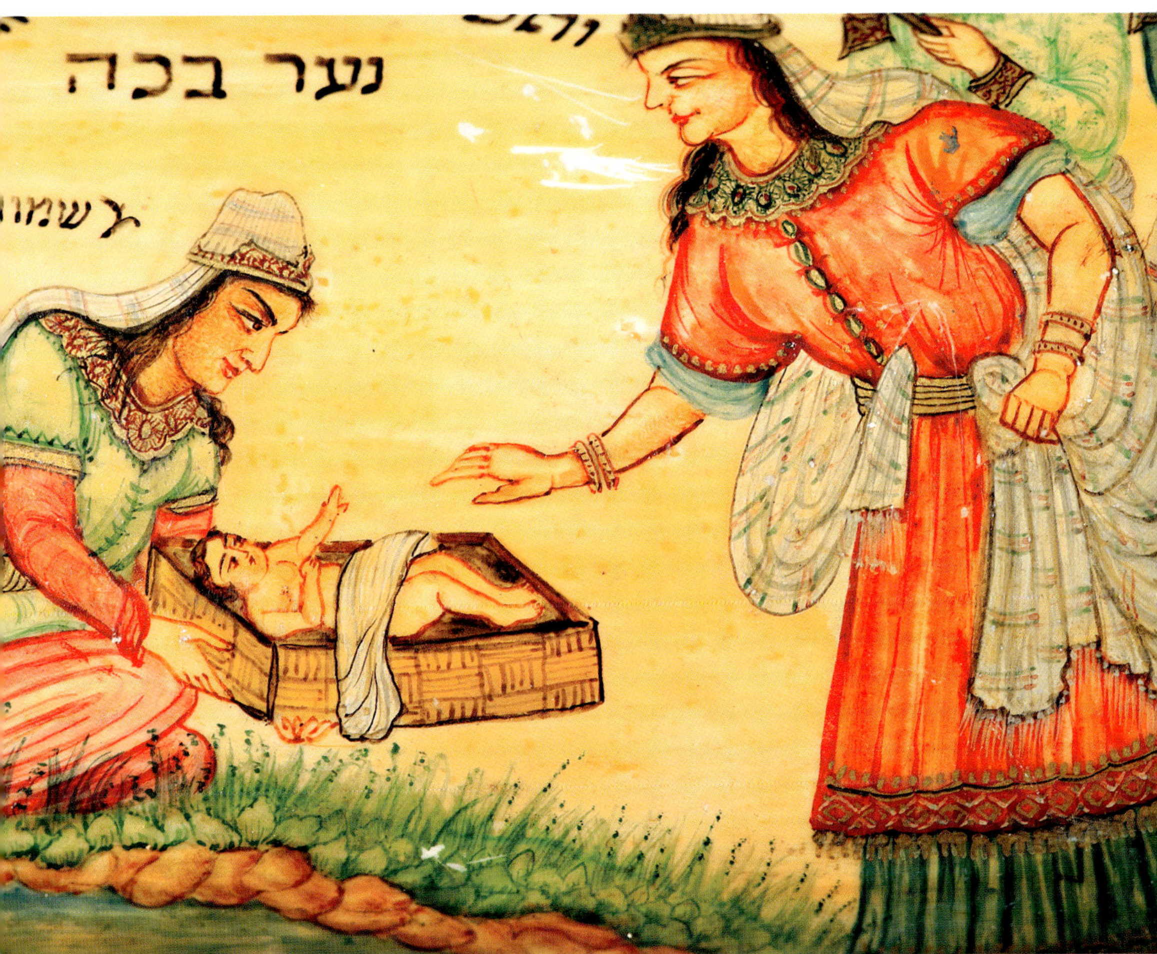

Wall hanging, 1985

Islamic

Acrylic velvet, 178 × 218.5 cm

Gift from Ameena Mughal, 2011

LEEDM.F.2012.5.1

This picture cloth carries a dramatic depiction of the Hajj, the annual pilgrimage to Mecca. It shows the mosque at Mecca, Masjid al-Haram, with the *Ka'aba* stone in the centre surrounded by circling pilgrims. Around the border are cartouches illustrating other Hajj pilgrimage sites. It is a statement piece – over two metres in width – and it was made as a souvenir for pilgrims to take home after Hajj. It belonged to Rozama Bibi, of Bradford, who bought it in a souvenir shop in Mecca after her Hajj in 1985. It was donated by her granddaughter Ameena Mughal, a former student intern working on our *Voices of Asia* gallery, who remembers it displayed on her grandmother's living room wall.

The Hajj is one of the five pillars of Islam which every able-bodied and financially capable Muslim must undertake at least once in their lifetime. It attracts some three million pilgrims who undertake a series of rituals over the course of four days: walking anti-clockwise seven times around the *Ka'aba*; drinking from the *Zamzam* well; standing vigil on the plains of Mount Arafat; and throwing stones in a ritual stoning of the Devil. Finally, the pilgrims shave their heads and perform an animal sacrifice; only then may they celebrate the three-day festival of *Eid al-Adha*.

The pilgrimage has become a major cultural and social institution, uniting Muslims regardless of ethnicity or sect. It touches the lives of all Muslims living in our city, and in 2011–12 we participated in the British Museum *Hajj: into the heart of Islam*, where we invited a number of people who joined the Hajj to share their stories with us for a display in the City Museum.

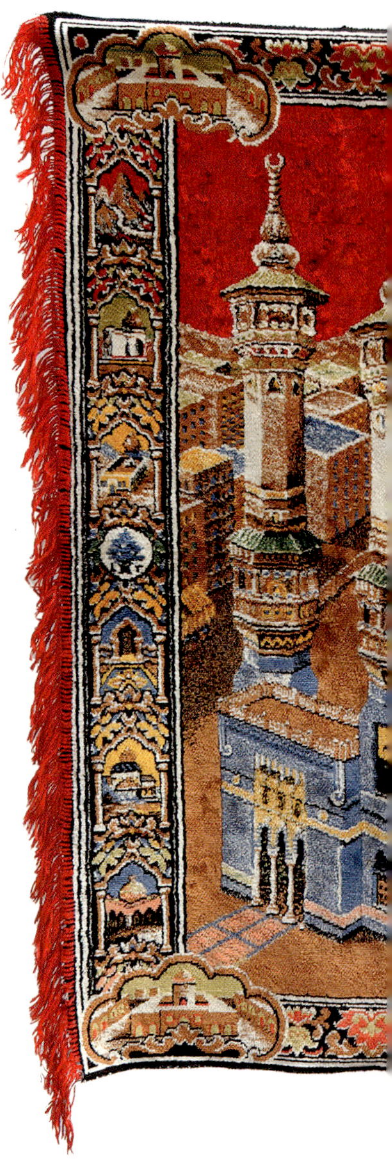

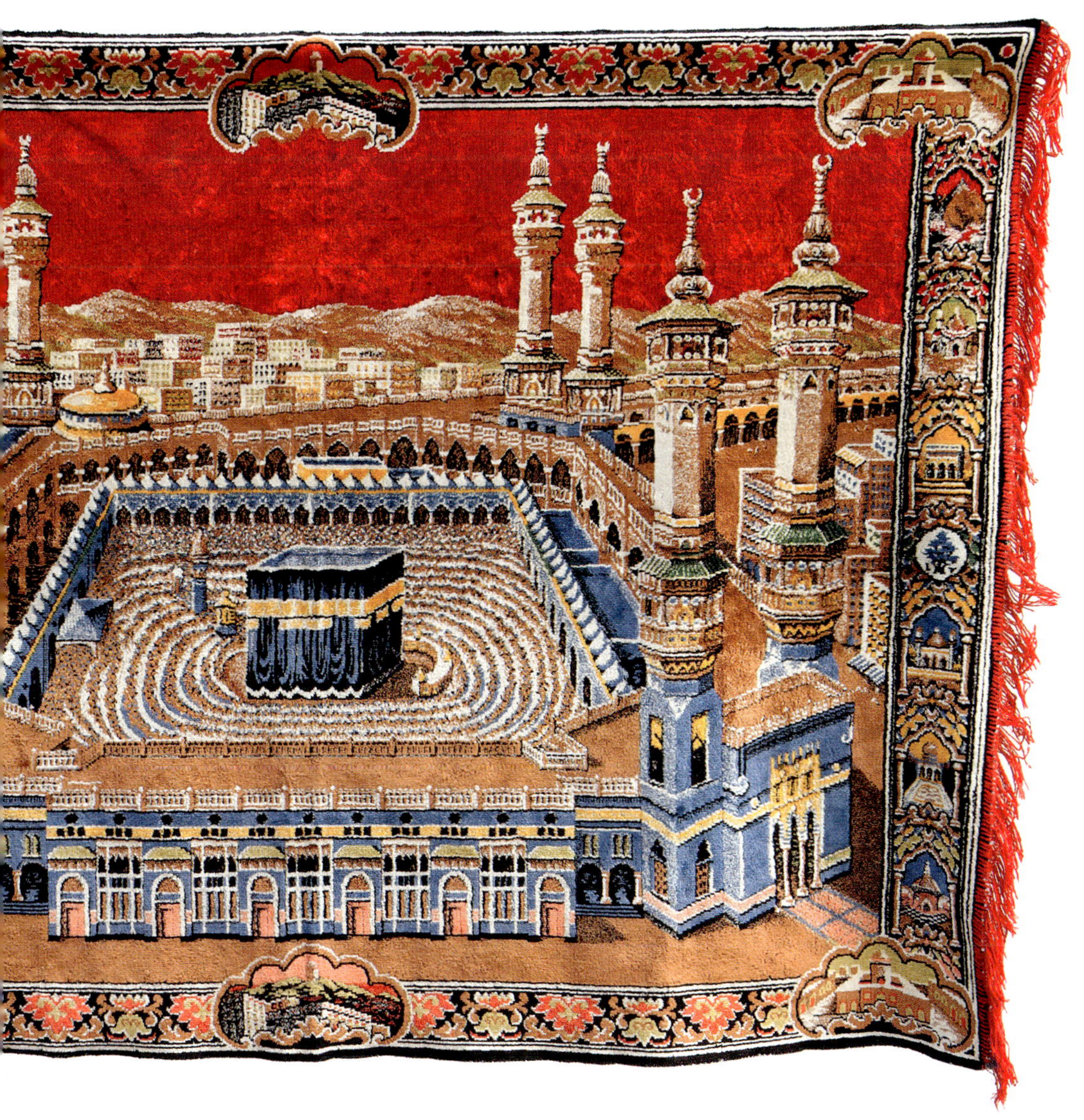

Paralympic wheelchair rugby wheel guard, 2012

Canadian Wheelchair Rugby team

Plastic, carbon alloy, rubber, ink, 55 cm diameter

Gift from the Canadian Paralympic Wheelchair Rugby Team, 2012

LEEDM.E.2013.31.2

Our collections in Leeds have grown over almost 200 years and through them we explore many things past; personalities, civilisations, habitats and cultures. However, we are also a museum service that recognises the importance of safeguarding the present if we are to continue the work of our forebears. Contemporary collecting and community engagement are key areas of our work and the way by which we involve people here and now in shaping our collections.

The London 2012 Olympic and Paralympic Games was an incredible opportunity to put this ethos into action. Leeds, I'm sure, like many other cities, embraced the games and the possibilities it offered for participation: the torch relays, the big screen broadcasts, the cultural Olympiad and, in our case, offering up our city's facilities for visiting nations' teams to train. Leeds played host to several teams from around the world including the Canadian Wheelchair Rugby squad, who trained at the University of Leeds in August 2012. When they left, eventually going on to win Silver at the games, they presented us with this wheel guard as a memento. It contains the signatures of all 18 members of the squad and bears the mark of its previous owner, Zak Madell. Its battered condition is testament to the aggressive, full-contact nature of the game, previously known as 'murderball'.

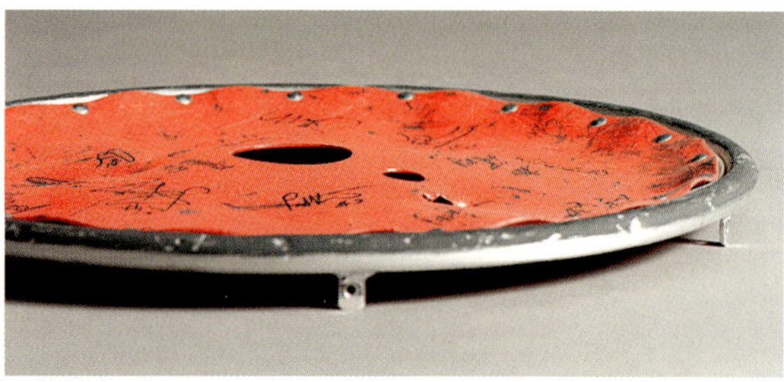

This is just one item among a large number collected around the London 2012 games. We worked with torchbearers, Olympians, Paralympians and their families, visiting teams, organisers, volunteers and many people in Leeds who were proud just to have been there.

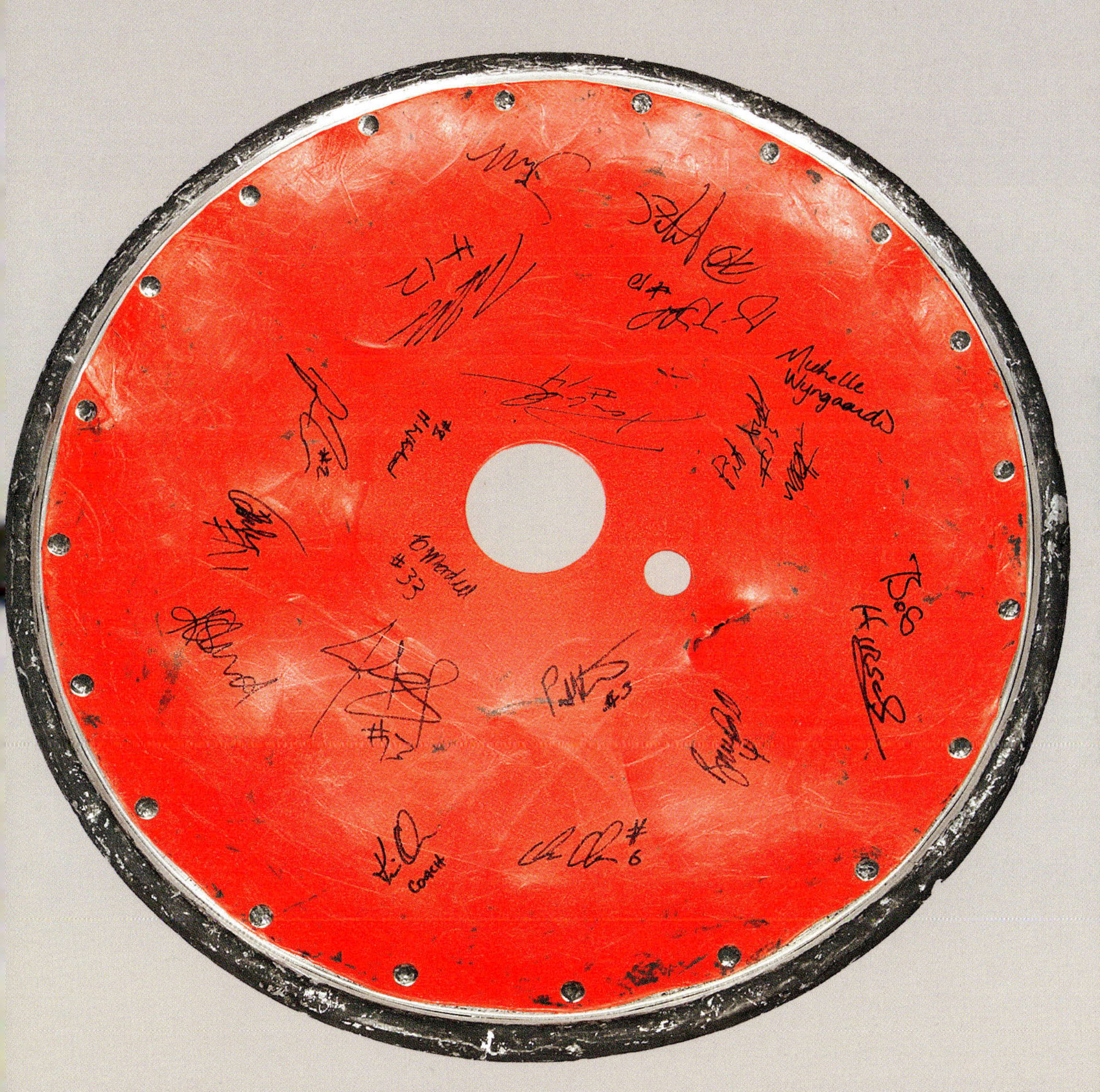
Michelle Wyngaarden
#33
#6
Coach

Ekoi mask, 1900–20

Cross River, south-eastern Nigeria

Wood, cane, hide, paint, 58.4 × 41 × 38 cm

University of Leeds, 2013

LEEDM.F.2013.2.96

THIS MASK, which would have been worn at the conclusion of a coming-of-age ceremony, represents a beautiful ancestress of the Ekoi or Ejagham people of Nigeria and Cameroon. The men who wore it were members of a secret society with sacred powers and authority. Masked as this celebrated ancestress they were adopting her fame and child-bearing success. The mask is made of carved wood covered in painted calf or goat skin, with a basket-work base. It has extravagant horns and a forward-spiralling headdress, black pegs for hair, black tribal marks on both cheeks and bone teeth. The elaborate hairstyle would have been the height of fashion at the time the mask was made. Several similar masks survive in other collections and in Leeds we have a companion mask, possibly of a male ancestor, which has small wooden pegs for hair and the remains of two large wooden horns.

This example is one of a large teaching collection of anthropological items which have been on loan to us from the University of Leeds since the 1960s. In 2013, arrangements were made for the formal transfer of these to our ownership, so we might share them with visitors on a permanent basis. Many of the masks, sculpture, ivories, bronzes, domestic items, musical instruments and jewellery from Africa and beyond came from the Wellcome Collection as part of its dispersal programme to regional museums. Anthropology eventually declined as a taught discipline in Leeds and the University loaned the collection to us so that a wider public might enjoy and learn from it. Many of the African items have been on display in the *Out of Africa* gallery at the City Museum and used to celebrate events such as Black History Month.

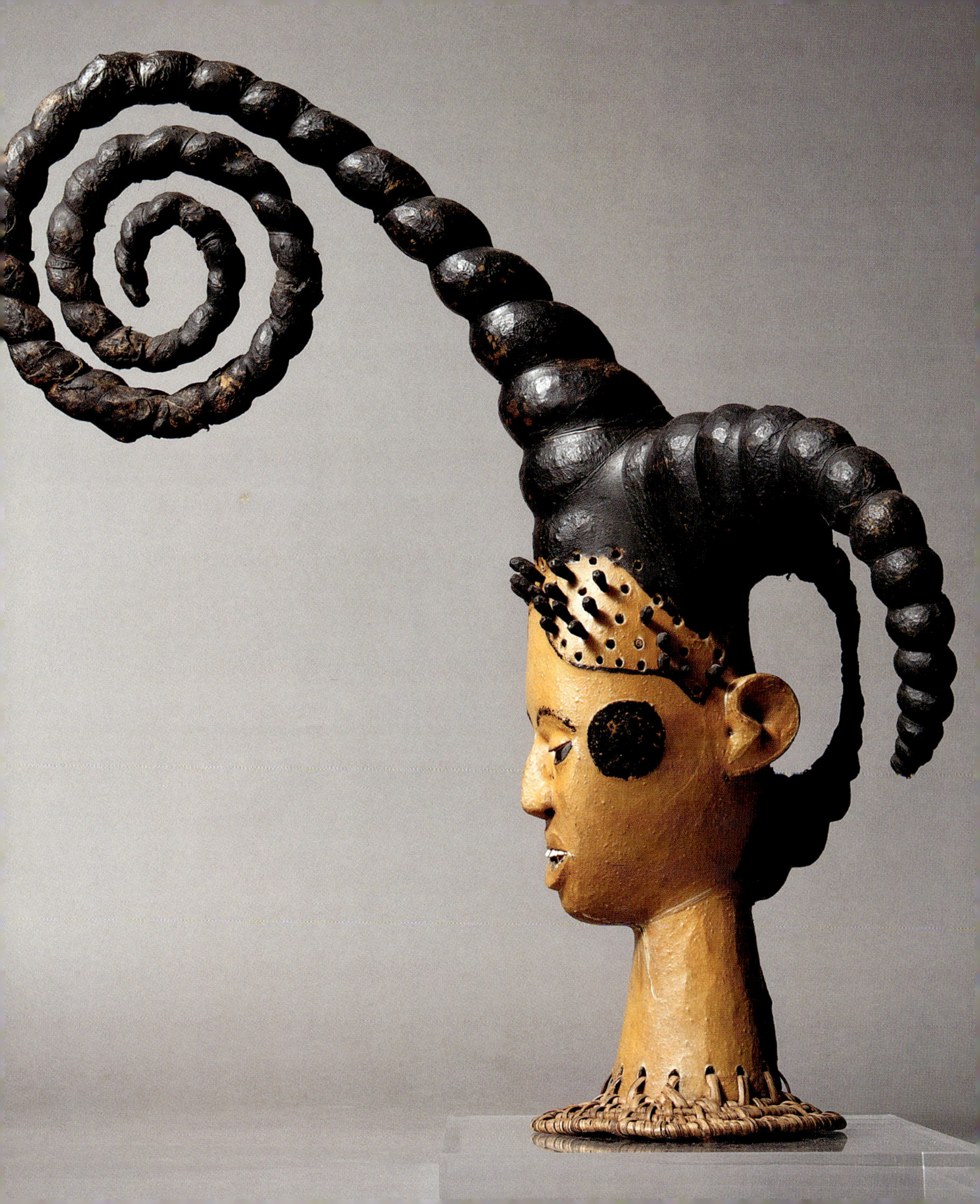

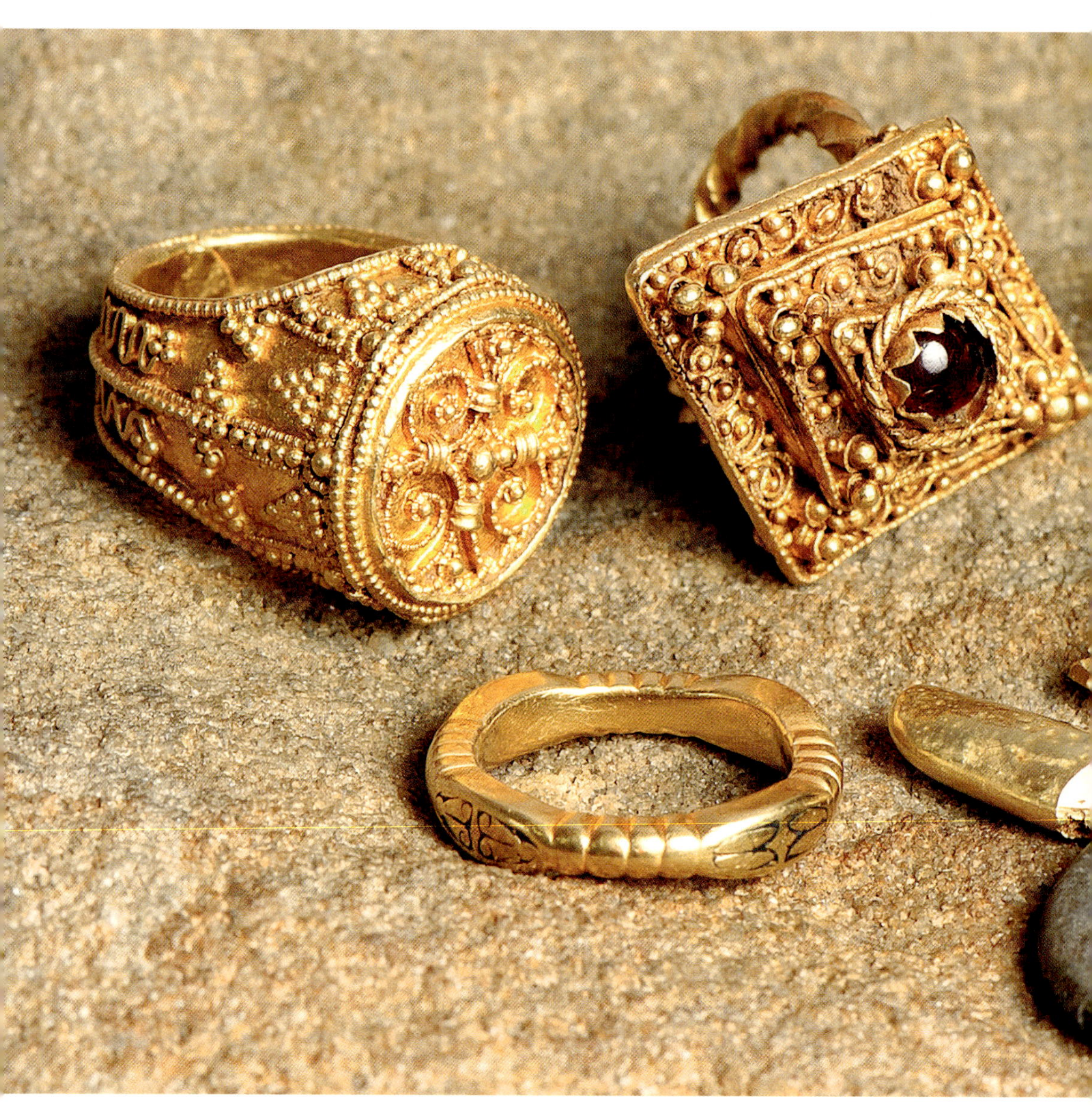

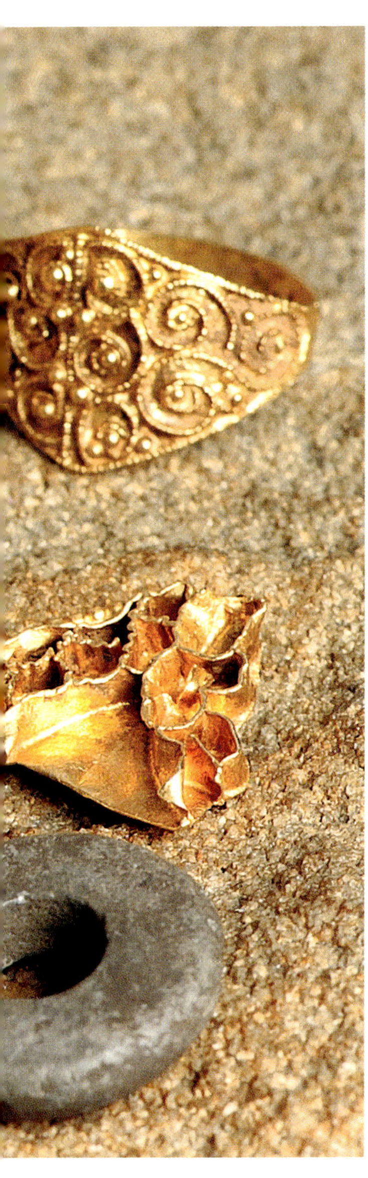

The West Yorkshire Hoard, 7th–11th century AD

Anglo Saxon

Metal, gold, garnet, niello, various sizes

Portable Antiquities Scheme Treasure, 2011

LEEDM.D.2012.1.1–7

IN SEPTEMBER 2008 a metal detectorist just outside Leeds, quite literally, struck gold. Over the next five months he was to uncover a hoard of early medieval gold jewellery and other items seldom found in this part of Yorkshire. The state of preservation of these items is extraordinary and the workmanship is the finest quality Anglo-Saxon craftsmanship. A public fundraising campaign fronted jointly by the LPLS and the Friends of Leeds Museums meant that this treasure was able to find its permanent home just a few miles from where it was buried some 900 years ago.

The most spectacular item in the group is a large ring set with a garnet gemstone. It was in all likelihood owned by someone of high status. Another ring is decorated with gold filigree and pellets, while a third, which is well worn, is decorated with flora and fauna in niello. The fourth ring is unusually large and is decorated with intricate spirals and twists of gold wire and granules. A fifth item, a fragment of cloisonné brooch, would once have been very fine and inlaid with garnets.

There is something of an enigma about this group of items as the brooch has been dated to the seventh century whilst the other items are later, between the ninth and eleventh centuries. There is evidence of minor Viking settlement across West Yorkshire and there is also suggestion of a royal residence where Leeds is now, which might explain the high quality of the jewellery. Whilst the purpose of this hoard is a mystery, various hypotheses abound: it may have been assembled by Vikings for reworking, or perhaps it is a thief's cache (the burial site had been disturbed and pieces of gold broken from the ingot and brooch, suggesting a thief returning to his hoard). The truth is, we will never know, but sometimes that is part of the magic of museums.

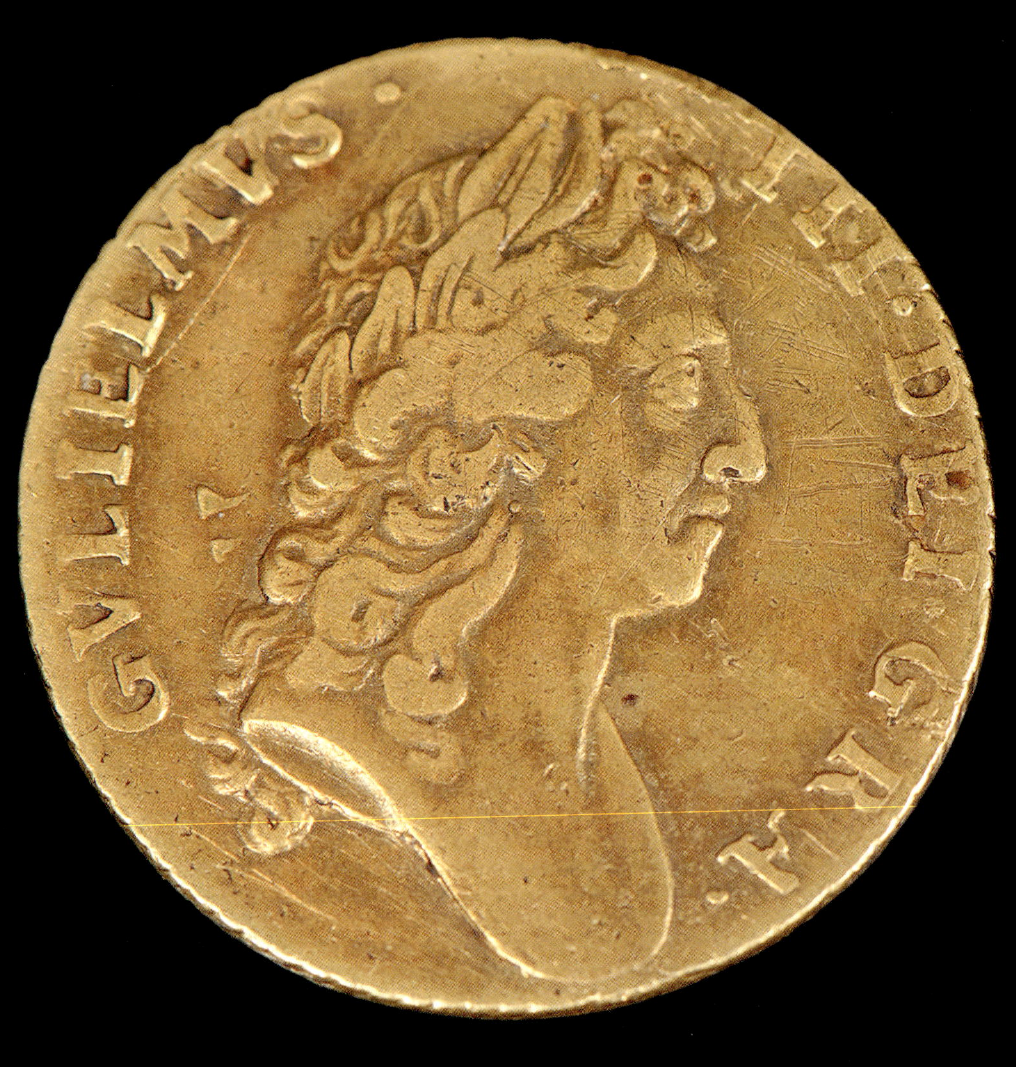
GVLIELMVS · III DEI GRA ·

William III guinea, 1695

England

Gold, 24 mm diameter

Leeds Philosophical and Literary Society gift, *c.*1872

LEEDM.N.2007.4.24

Coins have many roles – as art objects, as items of craftsmanship, as artefacts of trade and commerce, politics and monarchy – but sometimes the story of a coin simply as an object is just as compelling. This coin, minted in 1695, shows William III of Orange in full imperial Roman pose on the front; and the reverse shows objects of state – a shield, crown and sceptre. Its label reads 'New Bridge, Leeds, 1872'. There isn't a 'New Bridge' in Leeds and no records of any new bridges built in 1872. However, the Leeds Bridge at the foot of Briggate was renovated from 1870–73 and a 'new bridge' designed by Thomas Dyne Steele and built by John Butler Ironworks of Stanningley was erected, widening the river crossing from the previous 1760 construction. This 'new bridge' is still a principal river crossing to this day. Whilst we don't have detailed information on the excavation of this coin it may be that it was found by one of the labourers during the renovation works.

There has been a bridge on the same site since the medieval period and in the late seventeenth century a large wool market traded adjacent to it. This market became the centre for the wool trade for the whole of the West Riding of Yorkshire. As this coin's minting date corresponds to the growing wool trade of the early eighteenth century, could it be that it was dropped during the course of trading?

This small discarded coin reveals much about the city and two different phases of the textile trade – the wool boom of the seventeenth century and the expansion of the modern city as the Industrial Revolution took hold on the back of the textile industry.

Victoria Cross of Arthur Aaron, 1943

Bronze, silk, 4 × 9 cm
Gift from Benjamin Aaron, 1953
LEEDM.N.1953.125.1

This Victoria Cross was posthumously awarded to Arthur Louis Aaron, the only Leeds serviceman to be awarded the Victoria Cross in the Second World War. Sir Arthur Harris, commander-in-chief of RAF Bomber Command wrote to Aaron's parents: 'In my opinion, never, even in the annals of the RAF, has the VC been awarded for skill, determination and courage in the face of the enemy of a higher order than that displayed by your son on his last flight.'

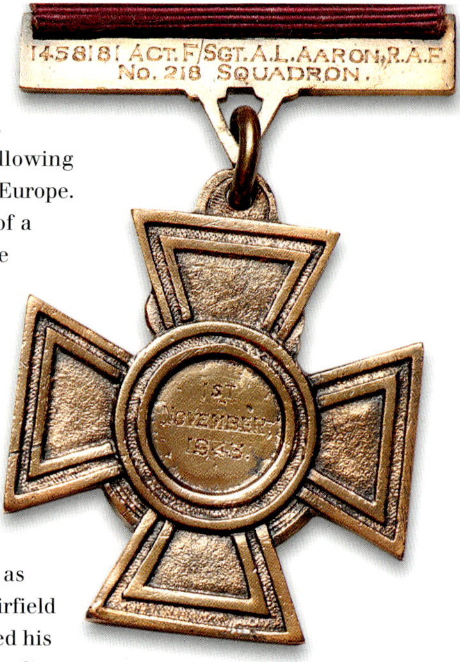

Born and educated in Leeds, Aaron joined the Leeds University Squadron before enlisting in the RAF in 1941. He graduated as a Sergeant Pilot and within six months was promoted to Flight Sergeant in May 1943. During the following three months Aaron and his crew completed 20 sorties over Europe.

On the night of 12 August 1943, Aaron was captain of a Stirling aircraft detailed to attack Turin. The aircraft came under devastating fire, which killed the navigator and injured other crew members. Aaron himself was badly hurt, losing part of his face and the use of his right arm. He lost control of the aircraft, causing it to plunge several thousand feet before it was brought under control by the flight engineer. Though in great pain and suffering from exhaustion, Aaron's sense of duty was undiminished and he wrote directions for his crew with his left hand, guiding them southwards to safety in North Africa. After resting, Aaron rallied and, mindful of his responsibility as captain, insisted on returning to the pilot's cockpit. Bône airfield in Algeria eventually came into view and Aaron summoned his failing strength to direct his crew in the hazardous task of landing the damaged aircraft in the darkness. Nine hours after landing, Flight Sergeant Aaron died from exhaustion. He was buried at Bône Military Cemetery with full military honours.

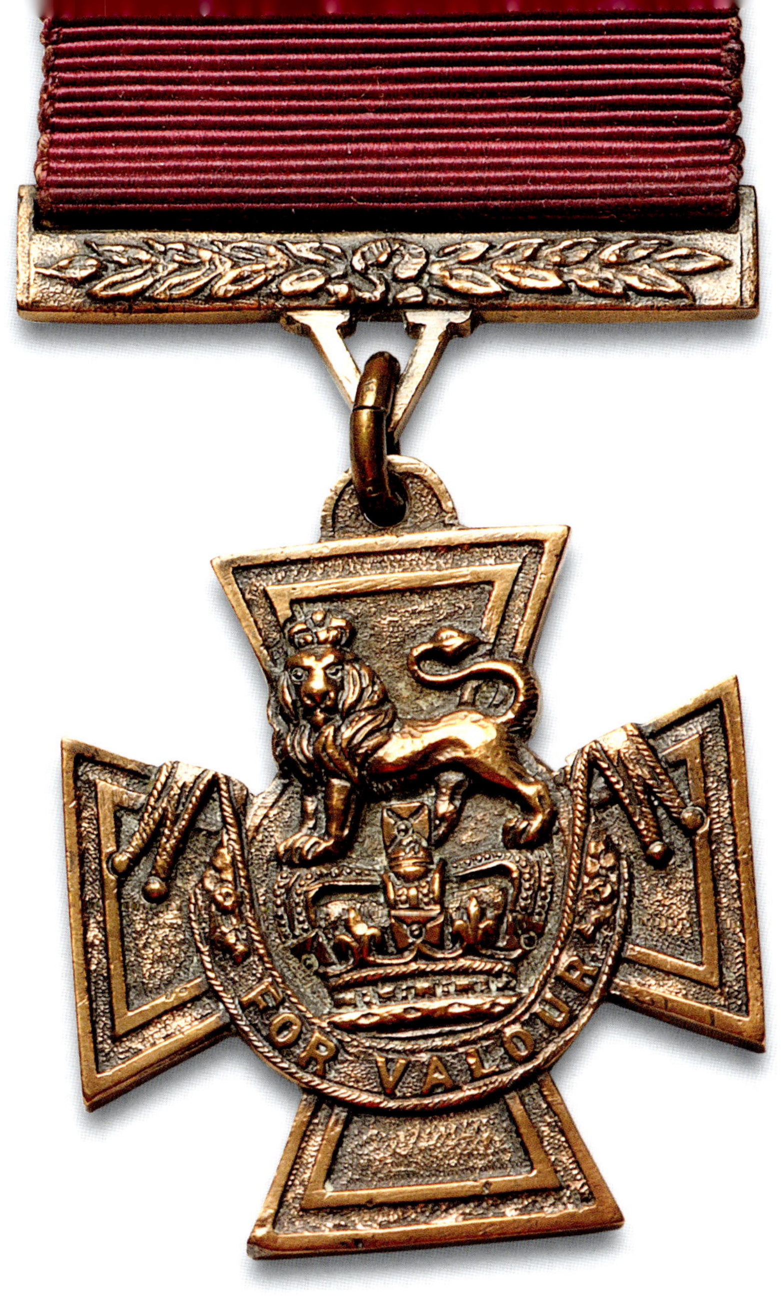
FOR VALOUR

Telephone receivers

Charles S. & James E. Bedford, 1876

Wood, metal, 17.5 × 8.5 cm

Gift from James E. Bedford, late 19th century

LEEDM.E.2011.309.1

These are actually part of the equipment, made and donated by James E. Bedford, a former Lord Mayor of Leeds, through which the first ever telephone conversation passed in the UK. They are now resident at Abbey House Museum, our social history museum in the grounds of Kirkstall Abbey.

In 2010 we had an enquiry from a descendant of James's brother, Charles S. Bedford, asking to see what was reputed to be 'the first telephone made in England'. Not realising we had such an important item we wanted to know more, but the evidence was still anecdotal. Later a letter from a volunteer at Amberley Museum helped shed light on the claim and included with it was a copy of an article from *The Telegraph and Telephone Journal* from April 1933:

'In 1876, he and his brother the late Mr James Edward Bedford, later to become the first Lord Mayor of Leeds in the Great War period, were two youths interested in all kinds of mechanical contrivances. To assist them in their hobby, they perused among others, the periodical *Scientific American*. From it they were vastly intrigued by a description of Graham Bell's new invention, the telephone, and they immediately decided to make two replicas.'

The first conversation over the line connected between an attic and a workshop 30 yards away was:

'Are you there?'

'Yes I am, will you count?'

'1,2,3,4,5,6,7,8,9.'

'That's all right. Will you go through the alphabet.'

'A.B.C.D.—'

'Wait a minute while I adjust the screw.'

It appears that the brothers just managed to make their replica telephone before Graham Bell patented his invention in England. Bell had been granted his US patent in March 1876. The Bedford brothers first tried out their version in October and Bell was granted his English patent in December that same year.

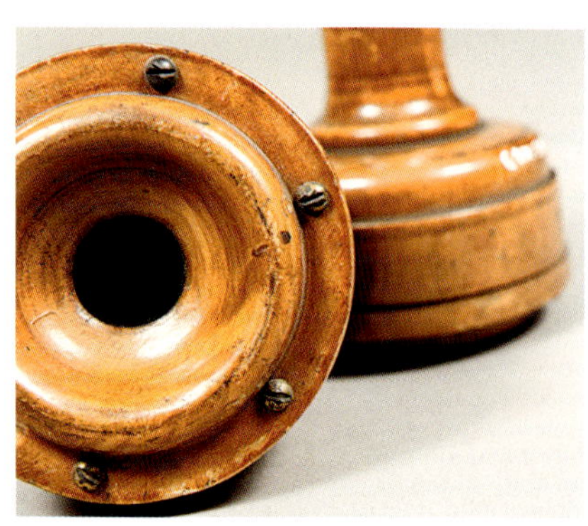

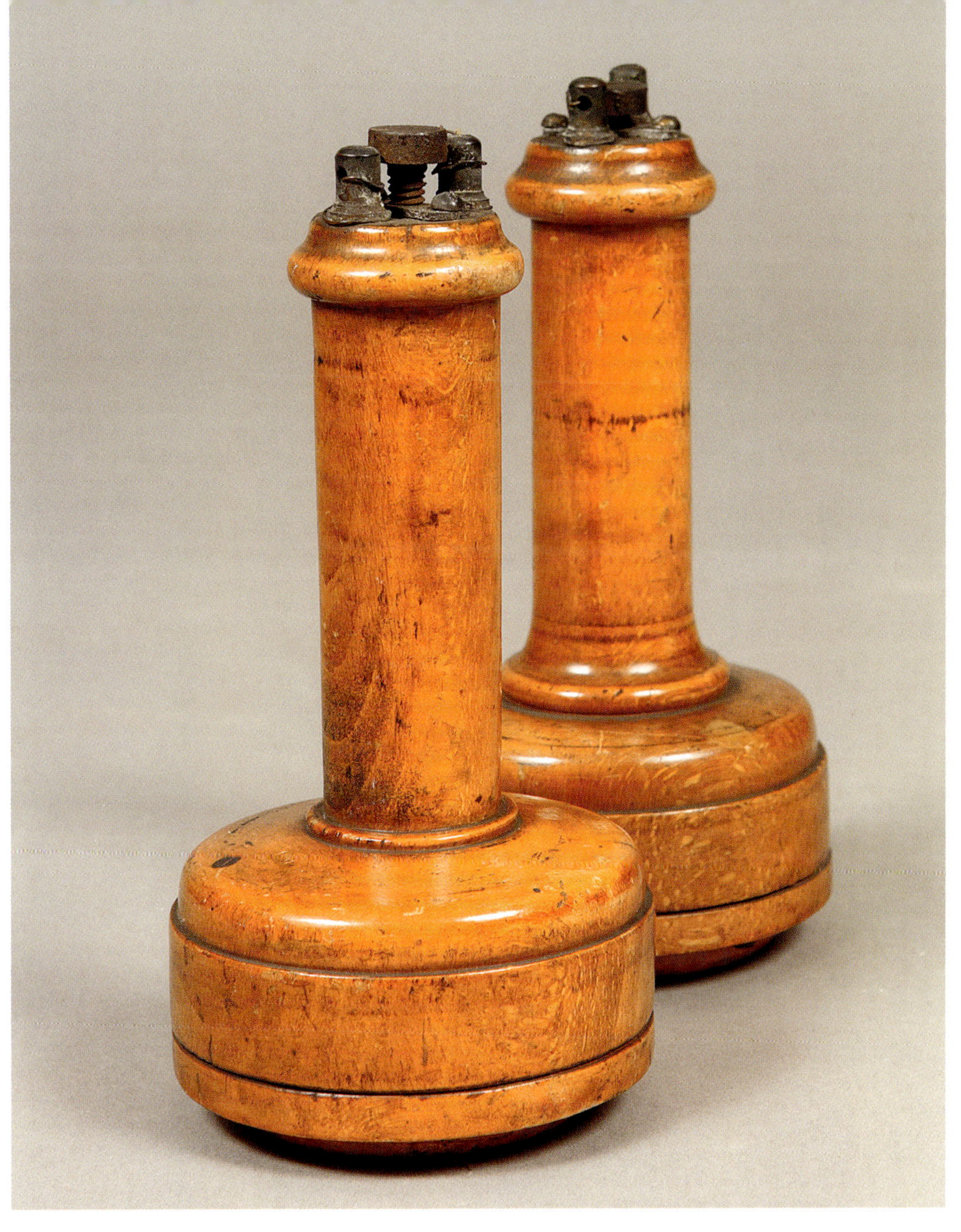

Hall vase, 1882

Wilcock & Co., 1863–1888

Glazed terracotta, 63 × 30 cm

Gift from Leeds Fireclay Co. Ltd, 1967

LEEDM.E.1967.31.12

This rather exuberant vase was made by Leeds firm Wilcock & Company in 1882. Based at Burmantofts in Leeds, it was one of the five fireclay companies that combined to become the Leeds Fireclay Co. in 1889, the largest in the country. All these companies started off making bricks and sanitary ware before they realised the potential of the art pottery market in the 1880s. These Leeds-made ceramics are referred to as Burmantofts pottery (or Burmantofts Faience) and are famous all over the world for their high Victoriana and eccentric designs. The company employed known artists to create designs for their art pottery; Edward Hammond, whose signature appears on this vase, was one such artist to be lured to Leeds.

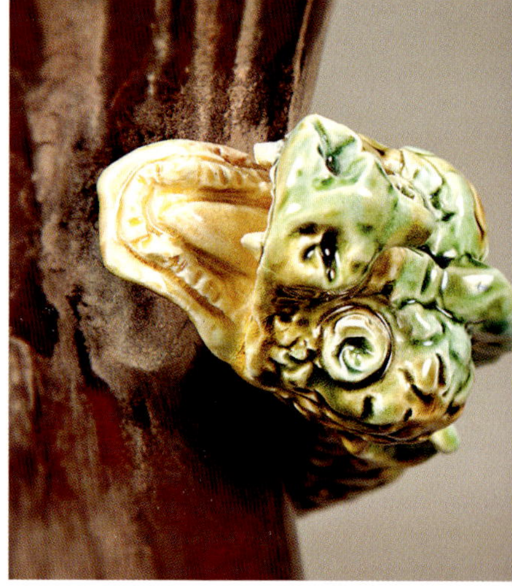

Fireclay was discovered in a coal mine owned by Lassey & Wilcock in 1859 and the company expanded their business from coal and brick-making to the manufacture of sanitary tubes and decorative building materials. Later they added salt-glazed bricks, fireplaces, chimney pots and drains to their catalogues. In 1879, Wilcock died and John Holroyd became the manager and it was he who saw the potential for glazed terracotta clay for pottery, branding it Burmantofts Faience. Business boomed and orders came in from around the UK and the world, including Paris and Montreal. Wilcock & Co. was briefly renamed The Burmantofts Company Ltd in 1888 before being amalgamated into the new Leeds Fireclay Co. Ltd. It made glazed terracotta until 1904 after which it fell from favour and the company moved into other areas of business, finally closing in 1957.

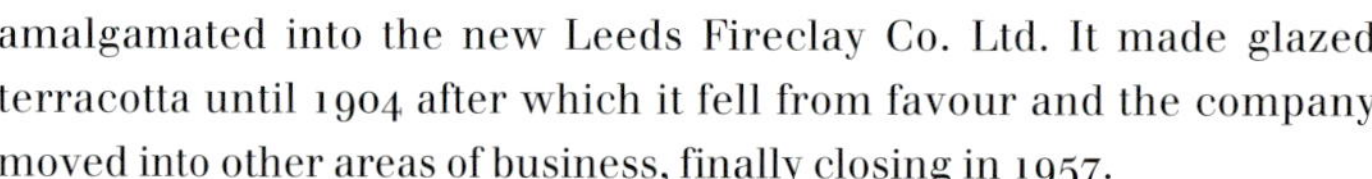

Burmantofts faience products can still be seen all over Leeds and give the city its architectural character. The most exceptional example, I think, is the Tiled Hall of Leeds Art Gallery and Central Library.

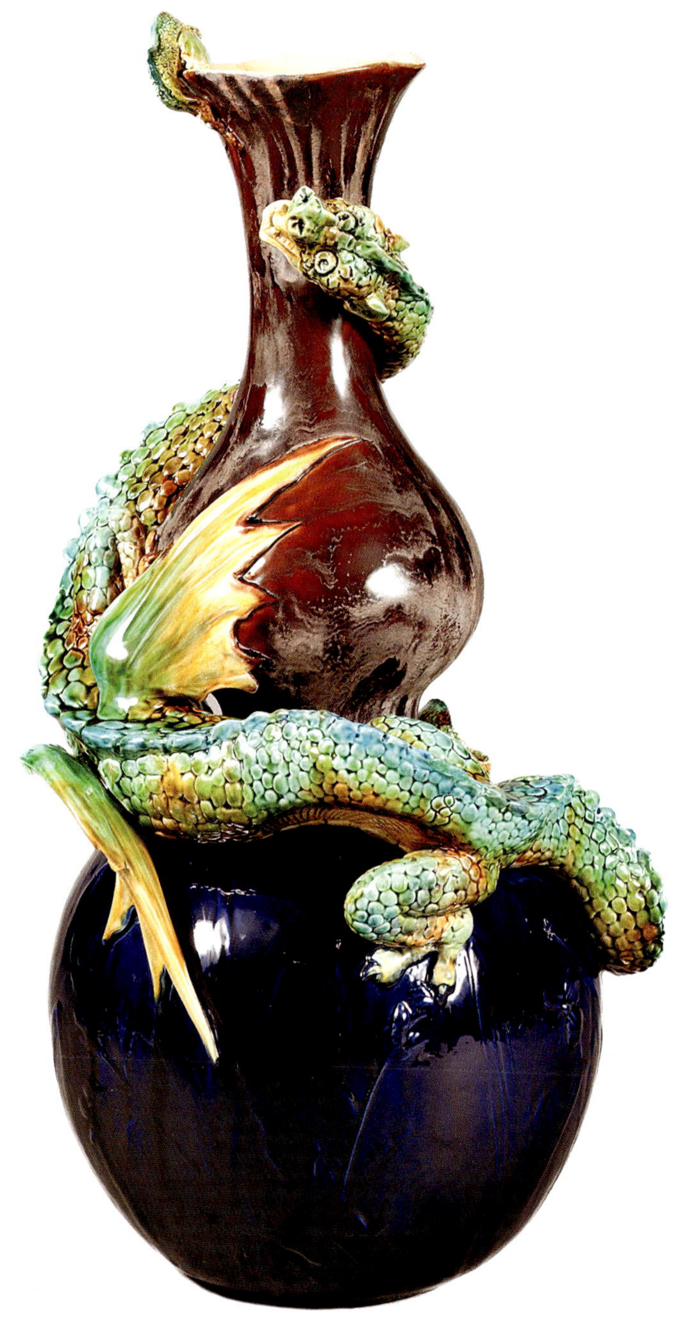

Suffragette dress, 1914

Leonora Cohen, 1873–1978

Rayon, paper, 131 × 110 cm

Gift from Leonora Cohen, 1967

LEEDM.E.1989.10.80.A

This dress was made by Leonora Cohen, who wore it to the Leeds Arts Club ball in 1914. Cohen was a formidable campaigner in the movement to secure rights for women, and one of the first in Leeds. The dress is made from green Rayon fabric with paper suffragette symbols pasted onto it, including a large figure of Britannia waving a flag which reads 'W.S.P.U.' The Women's Social and Political Union was a militant branch of the suffrage movement founded in Manchester in 1903 by the Pankhursts. They held demonstrations in London and other cities and published a newspaper called *The Suffragette*. The headline and pictures pasted to this dress are likely to have come from this newspaper. All are printed in the suffragette colours of purple, green and white. All in all quite a statement garment for a society ball.

Leonora Cohen was notorious for her direct action in protest against the government. In 1911 she threw a rock at a government building window and was promptly arrested and jailed. Undeterred, in 1913 during a protest in London, she smashed a showcase in the Jewel House of the Tower of London with an iron bar. The label attached to the bar read: '*Jewel House, Tower of London. My Protest to the Government for its refusal to Enfranchise Women, but continues to torture women prisoners – Deeds Not Words. Leonora Cohen.*' She was arrested again and jailed, and this time went on hunger strike. She was released days later in order that she might recover.

Cohen was eventually appointed OBE and lived to the age of 105, witnessing the rise of feminism in the 1970s. Once again, as a centenarian, she became a public figure and a voice for women's rights.

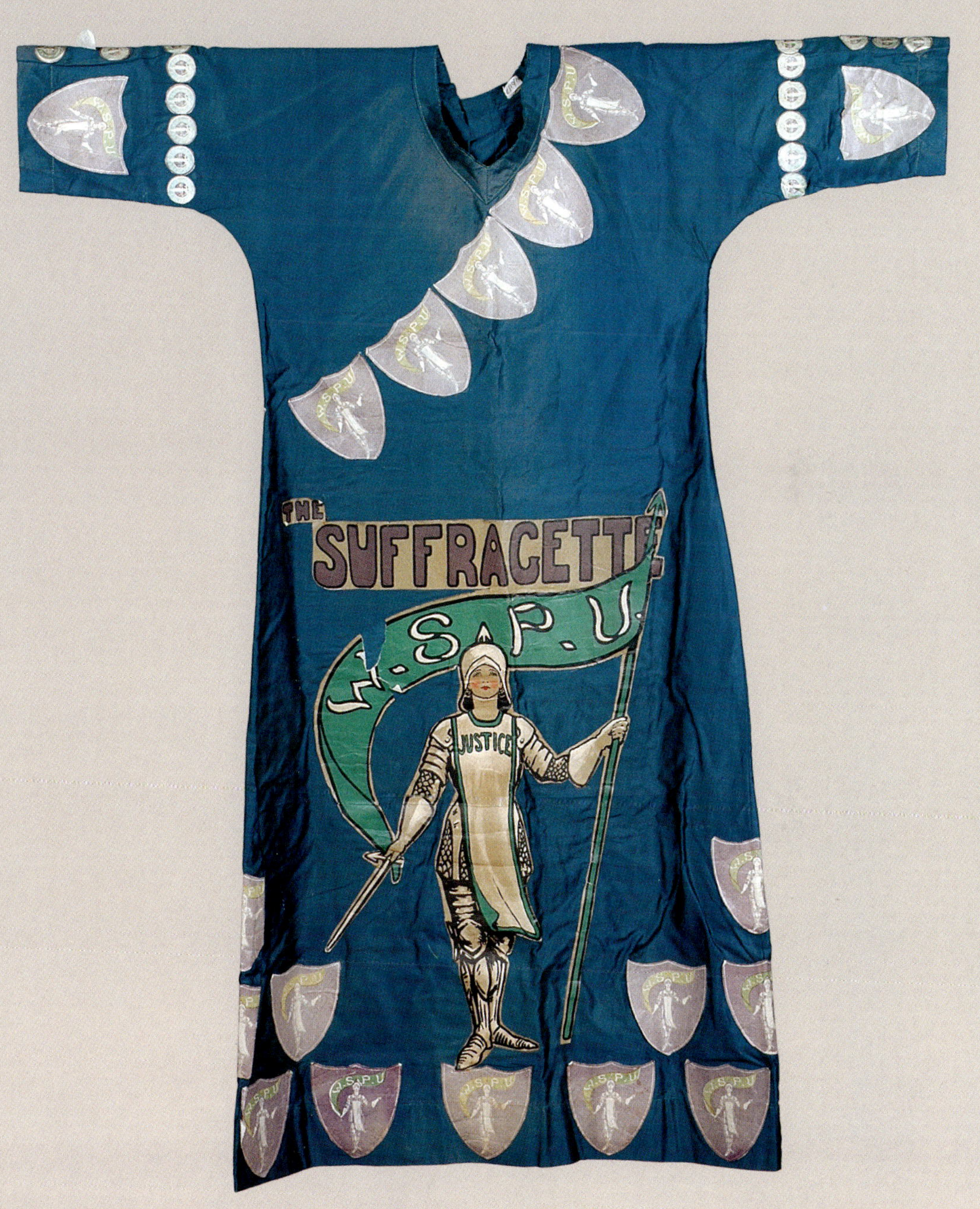
THE SUFFRAGETTE
W.S.P.U.
JUSTICE

Chinese silk banyan, c.1830–40

18th-century embroidered silk
Sanderson Collection, 1949
LEEAG.1949.8.145

THE LEEDS COLLECTIONS are characterised by some rare and fine items that say much about the passions and eccentricities of their collectors. Kenneth Wright Sanderson (1896–1977) cut quite a flamboyant figure in Leeds. He was the son of a boot and shoe manufacturer and, having lost his hand in early life, he was not called up for military service, allowing him to indulge his passion for historic costume. Sanderson amassed a unique collection of items, in particular, eighteenth-century costume, for which he scoured house sales during the early twentieth century. Sanderson was interested in the history of fashion at a time when it was not considered important and few people were collecting such items. He was a fervent advocate of the importance of history, frequently speaking publicly, particularly to schoolchildren (reportedly some 150,000), and also on the BBC's *Children's Hour* programme. He said, 'I wish to stimulate an interest in beautiful works of art not only from an interesting but an educational point of view in a city which has been called one of the most materialistic cities in England from a business stand point. There is too much thought of the value of a thing and less of its beauty or of interest.'

Amongst the fine dresses, corsets and accessories in the collection, there are many items of highly decorative men's clothing, which rarely survive, and we know Sanderson liked to wear them himself. One of his particular favourites was this banyan, which is an article of clothing very similar to a dressing gown and worn by men. Although the style of this one dates from the 1830s, it is made from a much earlier Chinese embroidered silk which dates from the eighteenth century.

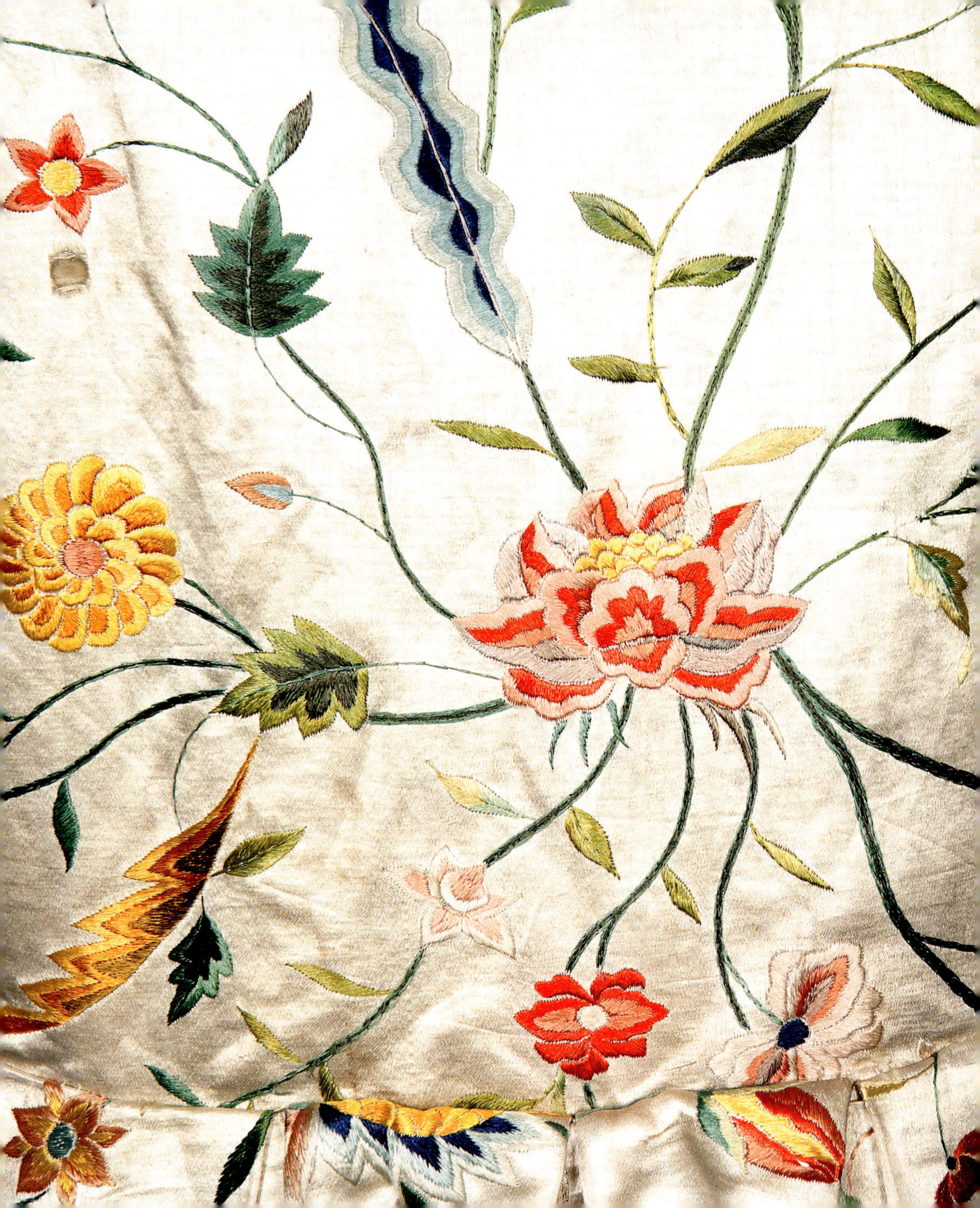

Scrapbook of 18th- and 19th-century textile fragments, 1975

Cora Ginsburg, 1911–2003

Paper, wood, cotton, silk, 33 × 50 cm

Ginsburg bequest, 2004

LEEAG.2008.131

At Temple Newsam House we have two exceptional collections of textiles: the Roger Warner collection of upholstery fabrics from English country houses, dating from the 1650s to the 1920s; and the Henry Ginsburg collection of European textiles dating from 1450 to 1900. The latter is a collection assembled over 60 years by the renowned American textile dealer and collector, Cora Ginsburg. Described as having 'an inexhaustible thirst for knowledge and a love of the decorative arts' Cora began collecting antique textiles in 1929. From 1950 she started dealing in textiles under the auspices of her husband's company Ginsburg & Levy Antiques of New York and in 1982 she opened her own gallery, which today remains the premier dealership for museum-quality historic textiles and clothing.

Some of her extensive collection was donated to Temple Newsam in 2004 by her son Henry Ginsburg, along with items that he himself had added to the collection. After that first donation Henry wrote: 'As the years roll by I shall be able to part with more of these treasured pieces.' The donation was to span a series of eight gifts over two years.

This unusual scrapbook was made by Cora Ginsburg for her son in 1975. This enormous book of textiles has a fragment or sample of historic fabric on every page, some clearly coming from larger pieces from the main collection. They are mainly western printed cottons, though there are some silk and embroidery pieces. Cora made it for Henry, perhaps to compare it with his own collection of eastern printed cottons. Whatever the reason for its making, it is a powerful illustration of their shared enjoyment for textiles, and in its permanent home at Temple Newsam we too can share their passion.

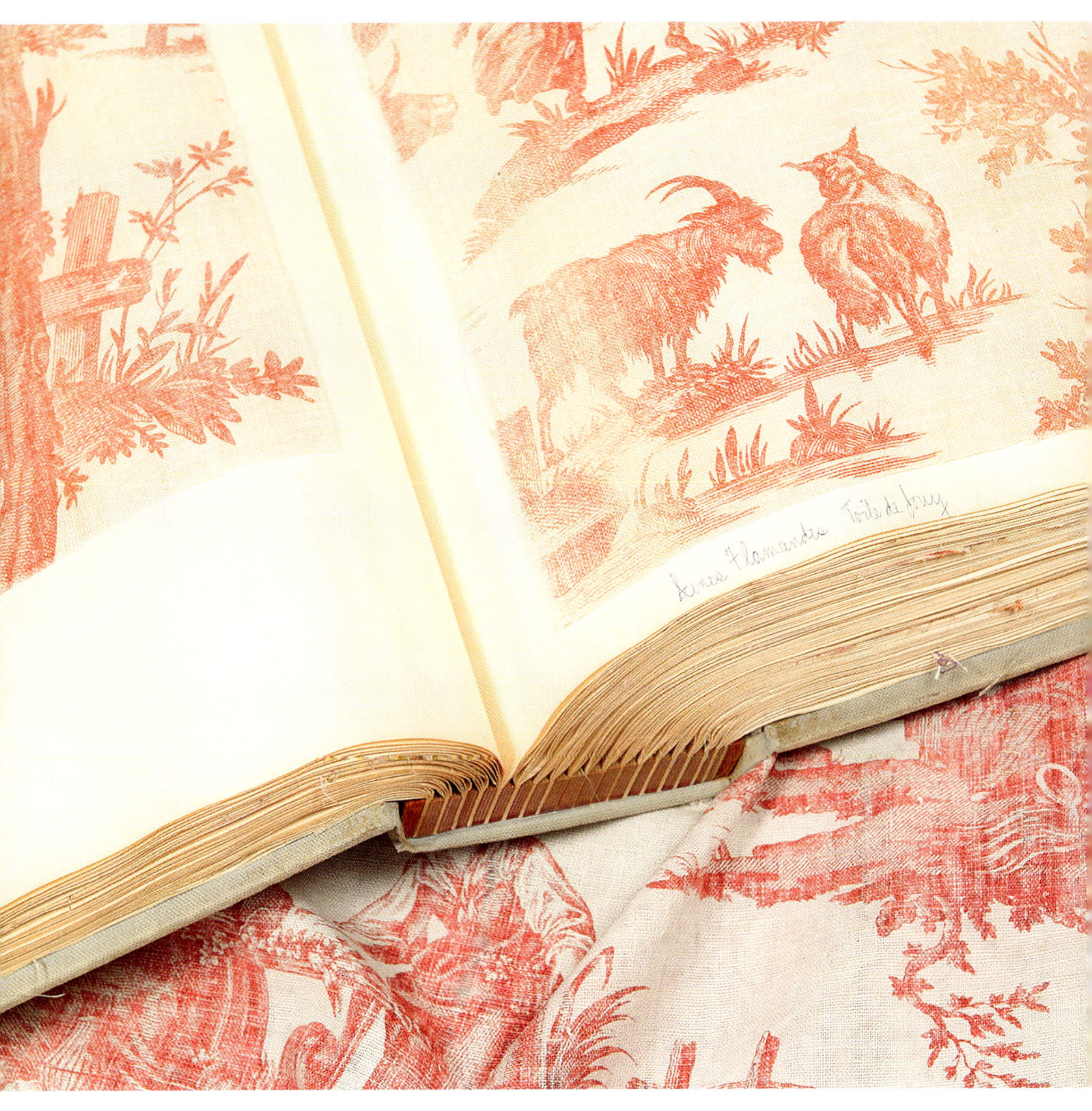
Scenes Flamandes Toile de Jouy

'La Belle Hélène' collection jacket, 1999

Dame Vivienne Westwood, 1941–
Silk, diamanté
Purchased, 2008
LEEAG.2008.18

The Leeds dress and textile collection is arguably one of the finest in the UK and it is certainly one of the most wide-ranging. With textile fragments dating from the fifteenth century to present day couture, we are able to explore the history of clothing and the textiles used for garments as well as for furnishings and home decoration.

This jacket, by Vivienne Westwood, is one of many items in the collection representing high-end couture fashion dating from the end of the nineteenth century to the present day. Other garments show the strength and quality of the British fashion industry, with items by some of the best-known British designers, including Jean Muir, Zandra Rhodes, Vivienne Westwood, Bruce Oldfield, Philip Treacy and Alexander McQueen.

Vivienne Westwood is known for her insubordinate and wicked approach to fashion. With its puffed sleeves and pretty 'cottage-style' fabric, this jacket seems a little too traditional. However, a closer look at the print design reveals a shepherdess who seems to have lost her top, much to the delight of her companion. Also the jacket is entirely lined with diamanté studs, which press against bare skin in a sensual way, making the jacket rather subversive, and very punk.

The fabric is of particular interest as it is a screen-printed copy of a famous design for a 1700s copper-plate printed cotton *Toile de Nantes* called 'Le Mouton Chéri'. Such designs were considered slightly naughty and really only suitable for bedrooms. An original fragment of this design is contained within the Ginsburg collection.

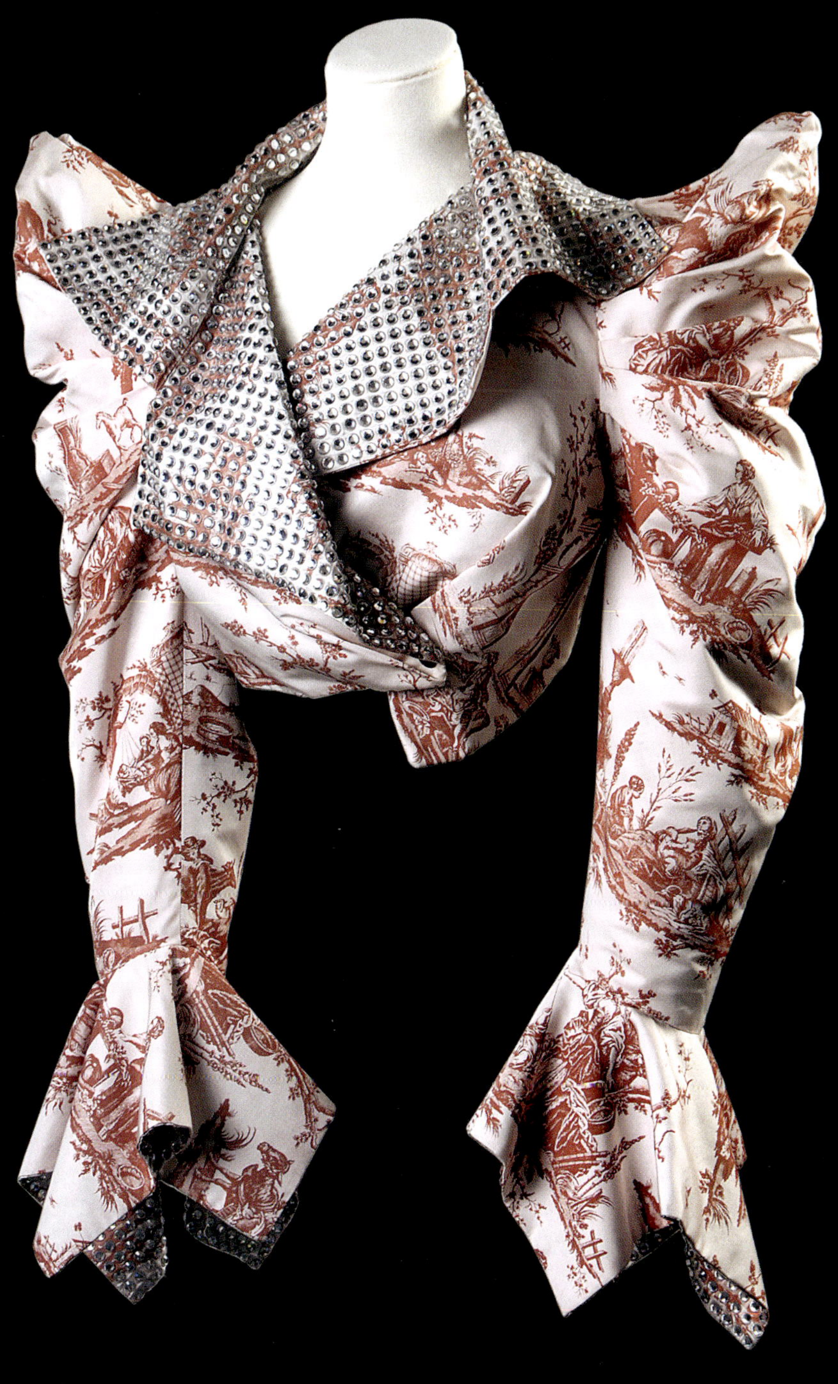

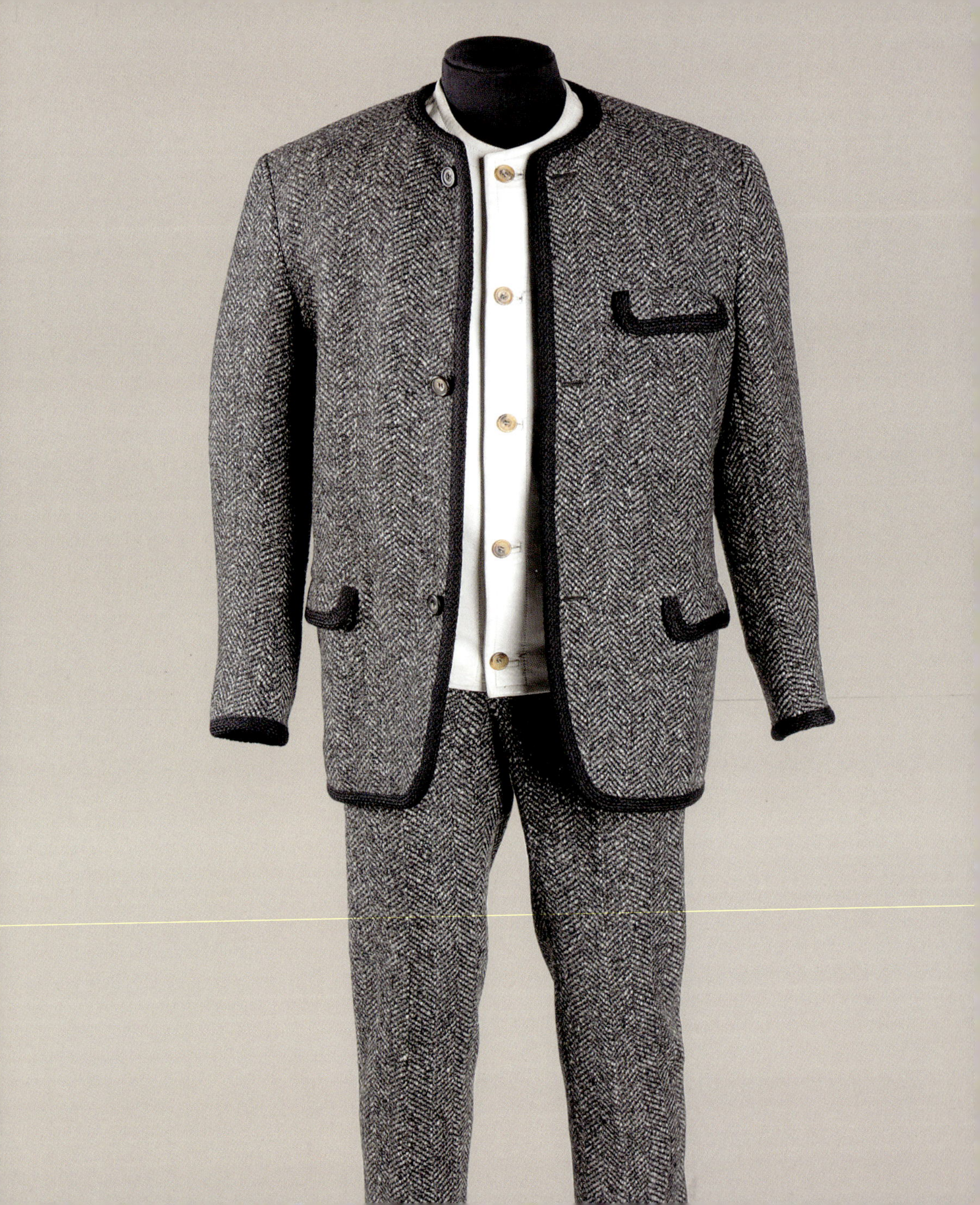

Man's suit, 1964

Hardy Amies for Hepworths, Leeds

Wool, leather

Gift from J. Hepworth & Son Ltd, 1979

LEEDM.S.1979.21.2

Leeds' important history as a centre for tailoring and clothing production for over 100 years started in the mid-nineteenth century. At its height the Leeds tailoring industry was dressing over half the male population of Britain. Leeds tailors were best known for mass production of ready-to-wear suits and also for pioneering the 'made-to-measure' suit. Somewhere between a bespoke and a ready-to-wear garment, the made-to-measure suit appeared at the end of the nineteenth century when the Leeds tailor Montague Burton was experimenting with ways to cut the cost of making a suit through the use of mechanised mass production. Burton was hugely successful in his experiments and other Leeds tailors followed his idea of 'wholesale bespoke'.

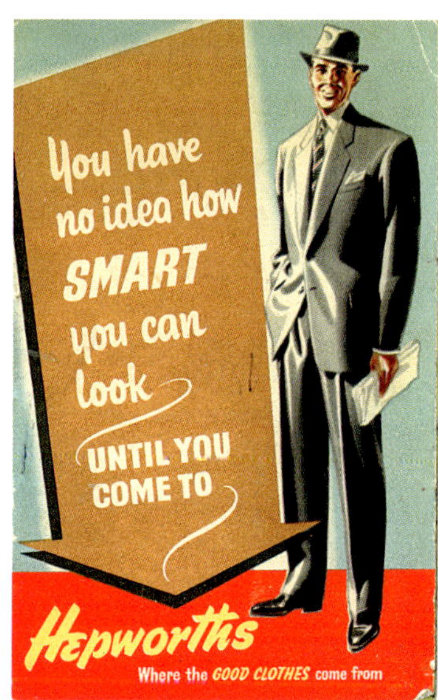

However, it was not just manufacturing – Leeds tailors were successful in retail too. Many of the Leeds tailors were what are known as multiples, meaning they directly controlled the production, distribution and sale of the suits made in their factories in Leeds to a network of shops they owned across the county.

The two largest and best-known companies were Burtons and Hepworths, and their shops could be found on the high street of most major towns and cities throughout Britain, as they are today as Burtons and Next.

This two-piece 'Beatle' style suit was made by Hepworths in 1964, the year the company celebrated its centenary. As part of their celebrations they created the *Centenary Collection* of tailoring, recreating male styles from their first 100 years and a collection of suits looking forward to 1974, of which this is one. The suits for the future were designed by the well-known fashion designer and couturier Sir Edwin Hardy Amies, dressmaker to Elizabeth II. This collaboration continued throughout the 1960s and 1970s, resulting in several iconic tailoring collections.

Self-acting woollen spinning mule, 1904

PLATT BROTHERS, Oldham

Cast iron, wrought iron, steel, wood, rope, leather, 153 × 1950 × 350 cm

Purchased from James Ives & Co. Ltd, 1980

LEEDM. S.1980.67

ARMLEY MILLS is one of two industrial museums in our portfolio which tell the story of Leeds as a city of a thousand trades. The other is Thwaite Mills, a former putty mill in the south of the city. Armley Mill was built in 1805 by Benjamin Gott and was at one time the world's largest woollen mill. It ceased production in 1969 and opened as a museum in 1982. The story of the wool industry from 'sheep to suit' can be explored at Armley as much of the machinery involved is on display, including two woollen mules. Both are by Platt Brothers & Co. Ltd of Oldham, one dating from 1871, the other from 1904. They are arranged as a pair but they were each acquired from different mills. The older mule is thought to be the oldest surviving self-acting mule anywhere.

The 1904 mule came from James Ives & Co. Ltd of Leafield Mills, Yeadon, Leeds. It is fully operational and is maintained by museum staff and technicians from a local firm, A. W. Hainsworth & Sons of Stanningley. The company identified that with some minor restoration and regular running, the mule could produce a high-quality woollen yarn suitable for commercial blanket production. As a result the mule is run twice a day to produce the yarn, bringing to life a 200-year-old mill at the same time as giving a boost to local industry.

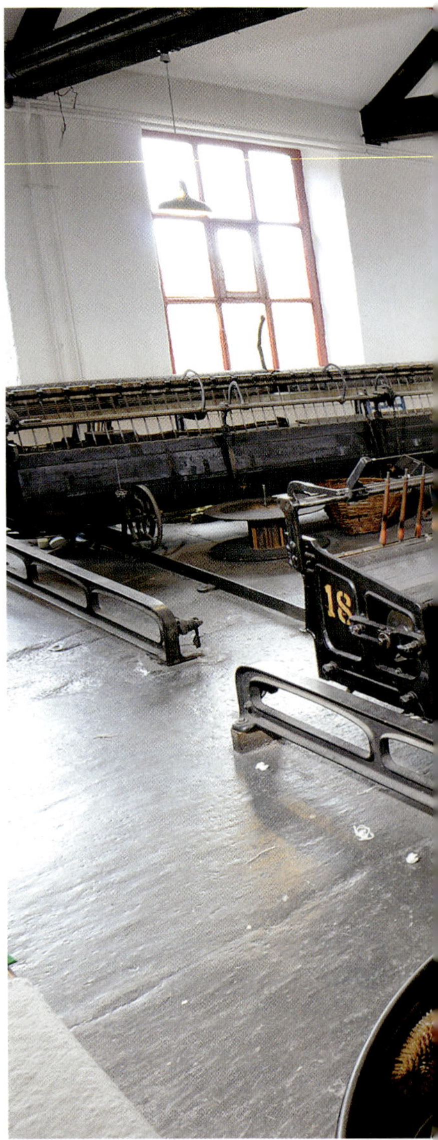

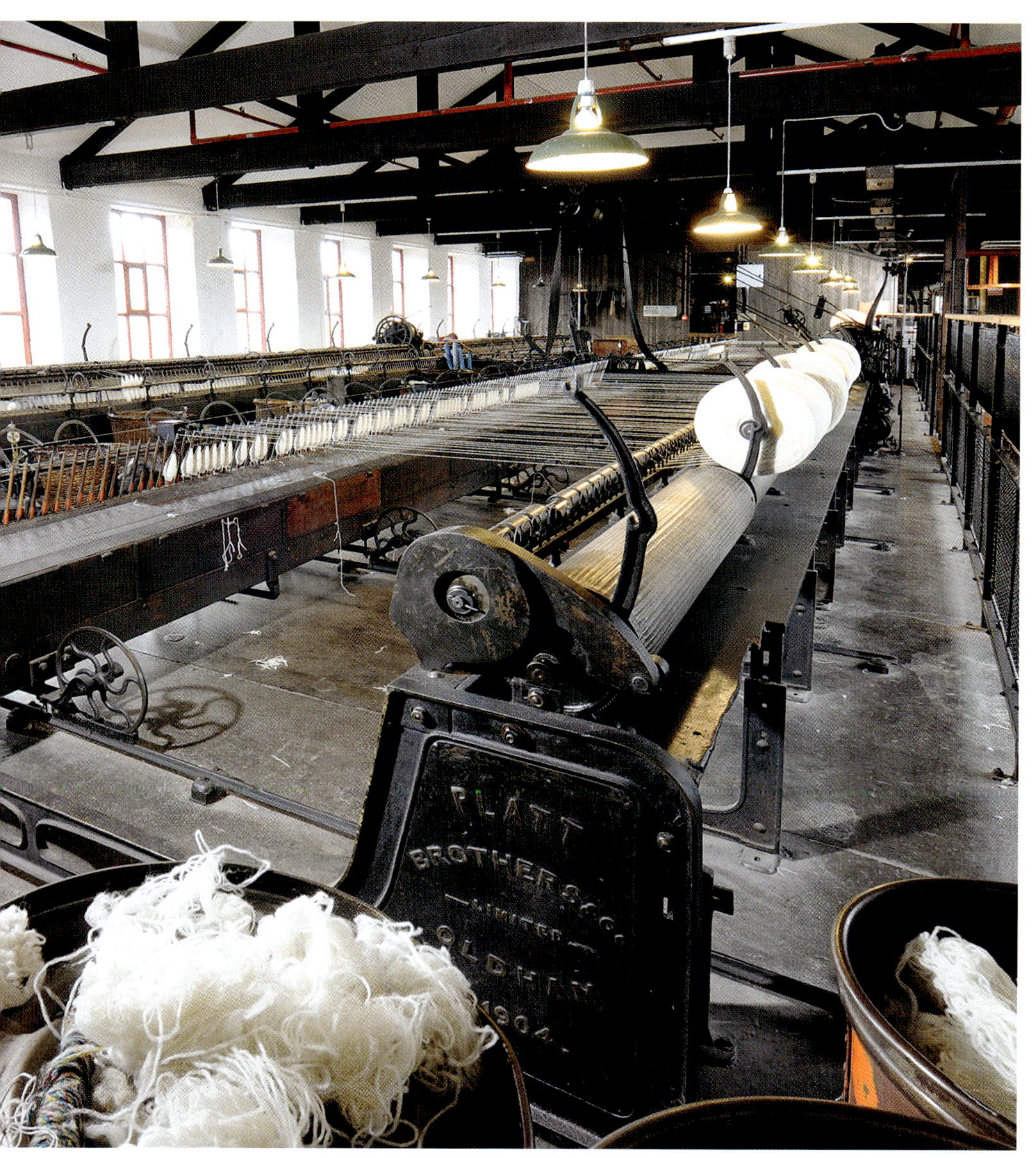
PLATT
BROTHERS & Co
LIMITED
OLDHAM
1904

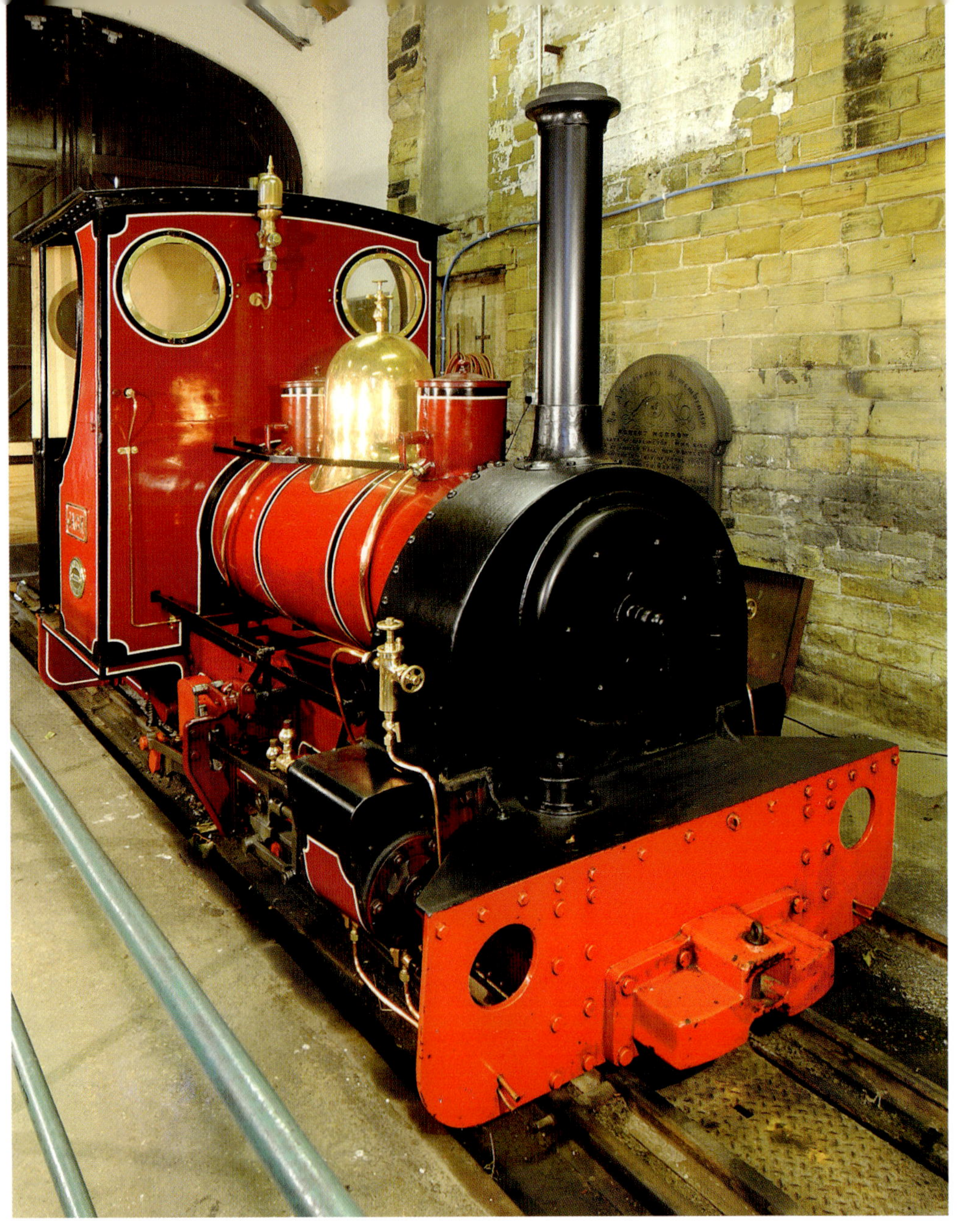

Steam locomotive 'Jack', 1898

HUNSLET ENGINE COMPANY, Leeds, founded 1864

Cast iron, wrought iron, steel, brass, glass, 230 × 390 × 160 cm

Purchased, 1958

LEEDM.S.1973.29

ONE OF THE MOST POPULAR exhibits at Armley Mills, home to a representative collection of Leeds-built locomotives, is affectionately known as 'Jack'. Ever since Matthew Murray built the world's first commercially successful locomotive at Middleton Railway in 1812, Leeds has been a major centre for locomotive engineering, exporting them across the world. Built by the Hunslet Engine Company in 1898, 'Jack' was one of only 14 locomotives built for an 18" gauge track. Founded in 1864 and still in operation today, the Hunslet Engine Company is a Leeds manufacturer making engines principally for industrial applications. We are also the custodian of the company's extensive archive.

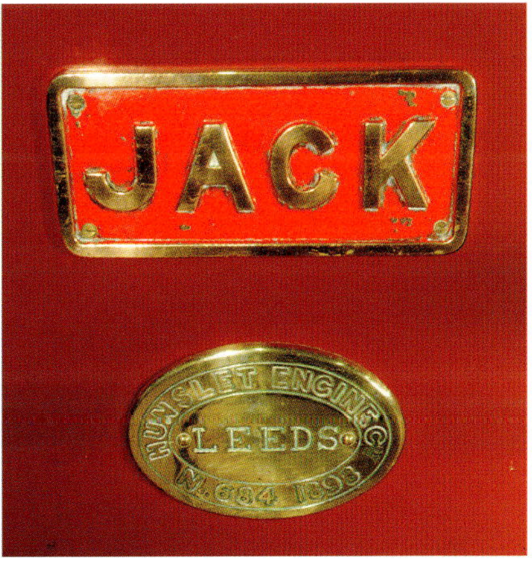

'Jack' was built for John Knowles & Sons (Wooden Box) Ltd of Burton on Trent, whose own track ran close to the Midland Railway lines, so 'Jack' was painted 'Midland Red' rather than the standard olive green of the Hunslet Engine Company. During the loco's working life it hauled fireclay to the kilns of Knowles' Mount Pleasant Pipeworks for use in manufacturing gas fire radiants. 'Jack' ceased working in 1958 and was bought by Leeds that same year. It had been altered several times during its lifetime and the 1898 components largely replaced, so we decided to restore it back to its 1924–28 condition in order to retain as many authentic components as possible.

A full restoration was undertaken in 1980 at Bradford Industrial Museum's Moorside Mills, which restored 'Jack' to full steam and it was able to run on specially laid tracks along the length of the Armley Mills site. In 2008 the Friends of Leeds Museums funded a final restoration of 'Jack' and he is now a tremendous spectacle on special steaming days through the summer months.

Organum Ptolemei, early 16th century

Brass, 13.1 × 0.7 cm
Gift from William Sykes Ward, 1918
LEEDM.S.2012.41.2

THIS IS THE ONLY known example in the world of an Organum Ptolemei found on the same instrument as a quadrant – a versatile tool for navigation, time-telling, casting horoscopes and a means to find Mecca. In the sixteenth century instruments like these were essential astronomical education tools – the study of astronomy being considered at the time a fundamental subject and competence in the use of these instruments a sign of good breeding and education.

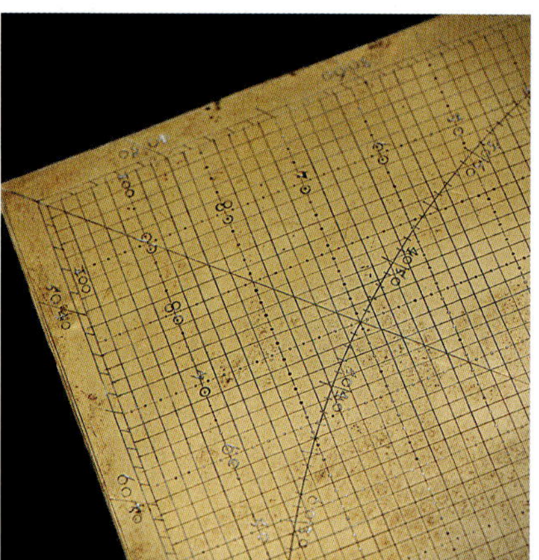

A quadrant is a type of astrolabe which shows the same projection as a traditional astrolabe but folded into quarters. Essentially it was a cheaper model which performed many of the same functions, such as navigational calculations. It would have had a plumb bob suspended from the hole in the corner. The Organum Ptolemei is an alternative depiction of the heavens as if projected onto the equator. It was usually used as a sundial but could also be used to plot celestial bodies.

This example dates to the sixteenth century and features two inscriptions to the obverse that both read 'Thomas Cock'. We presume he was the one-time owner of the instrument rather than an instrument maker, although there were many amateur makers of astrolabes. Working astrolabes were usually made from whatever materials were to hand, so an instrument like this in brass may have been as much an ostentatious show of wealth and education as it was a working navigational tool.

The Organum Ptolemei originally entered the city's collections via the LPLS in 1918 from the widow of a renowned collector of scientific instruments. It is one of several items in our collection that helps us understand the early progress of science and navigation and charts the advancement of science and invention up to the present day.

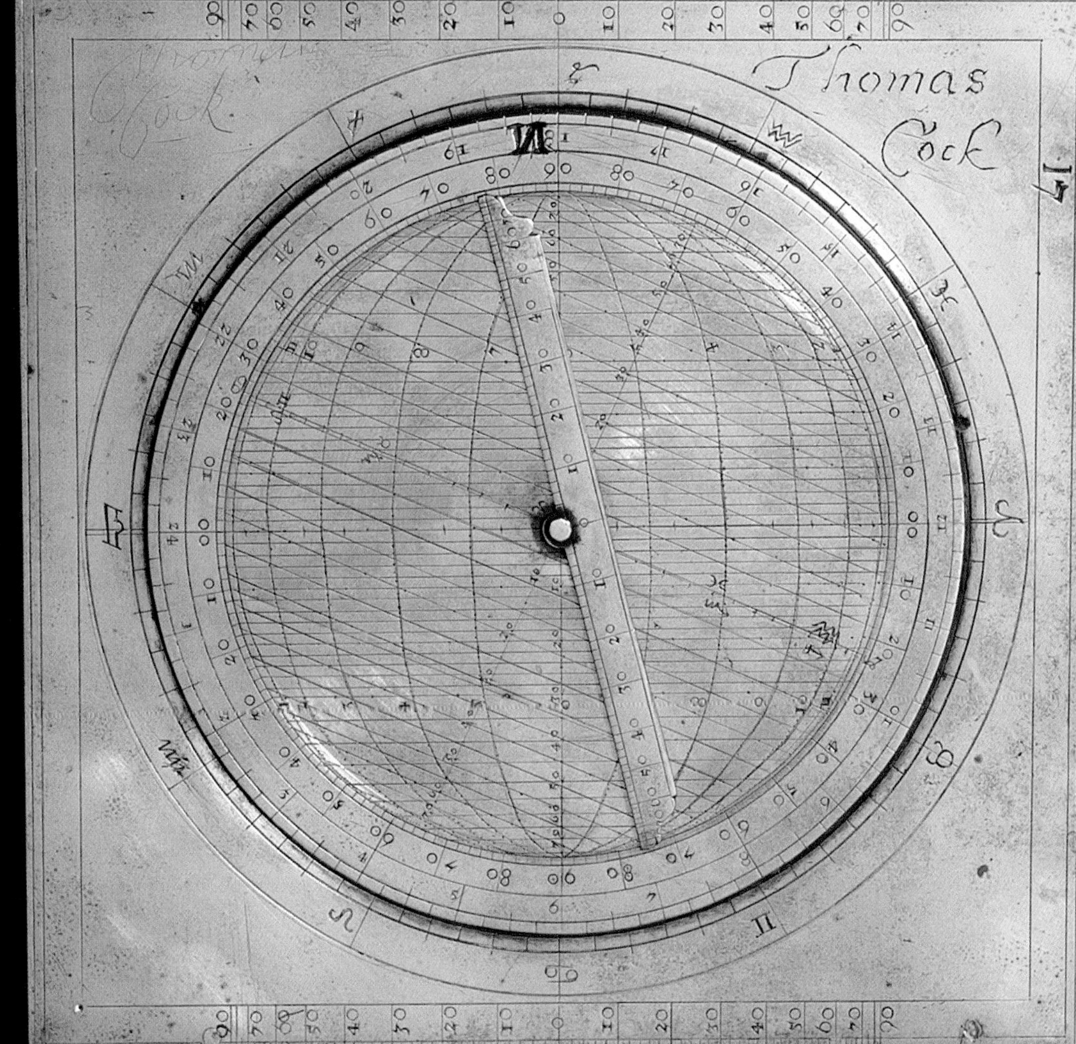
Thomas
Cock

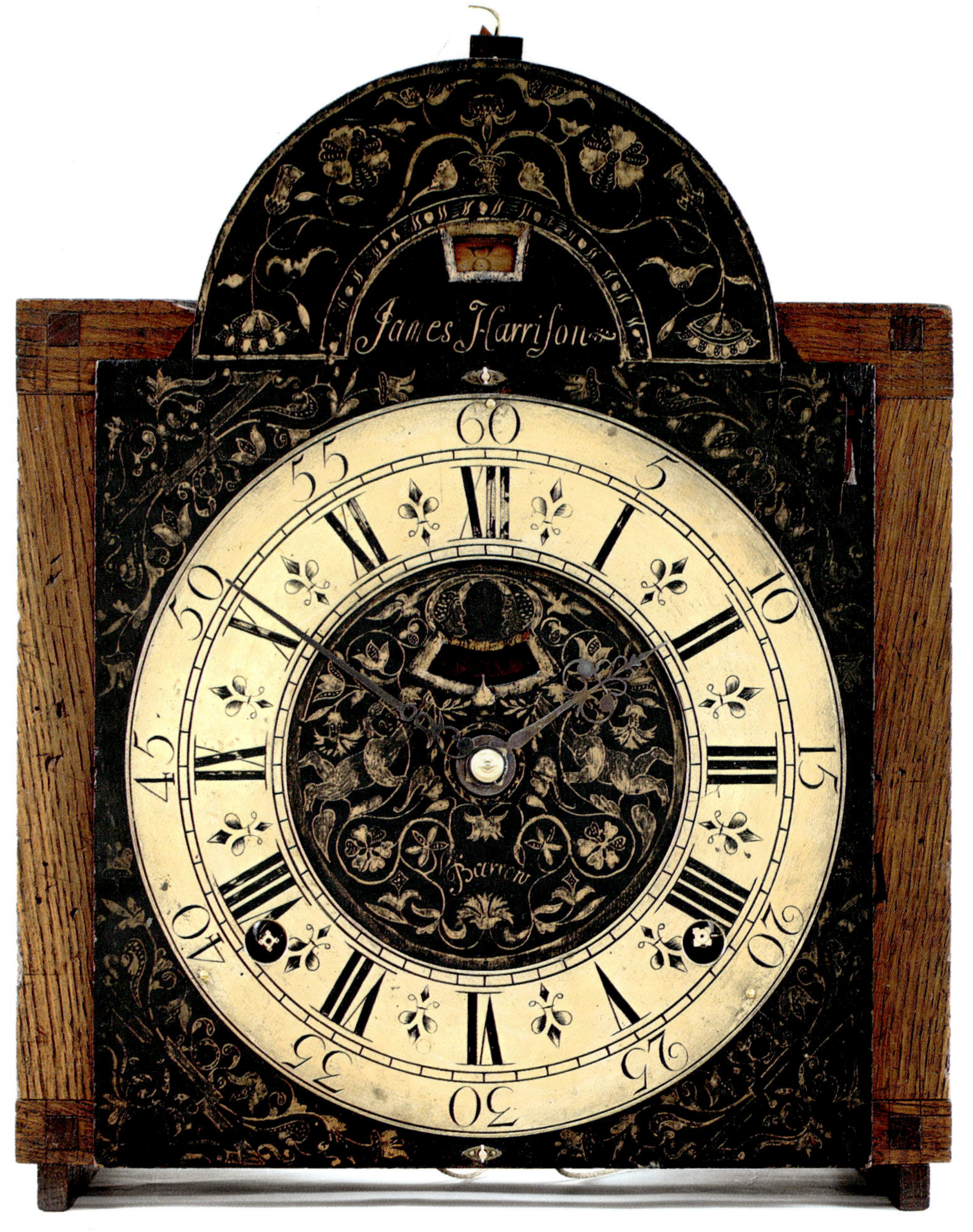
James Harrison
Barrow

Precision-pendulum Clock No. 2, 1727

John Harrison, 1693–1776

Lignum vitae, oak, brass, steel, paper, 218 × 53 × 28 cm

William Wyrill Sissons bequest, 1976

LEEDM.E.2009.99

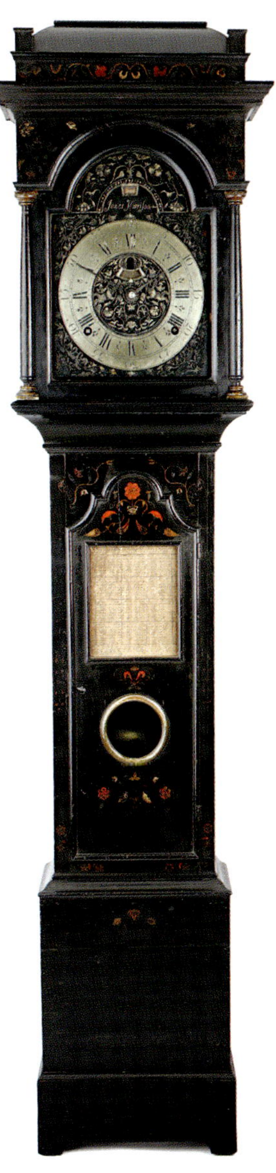

This humble-looking long case clock has a back-story that makes it one of the most significant items in our collections. It holds within it the beginnings of the answer to the Longitude Problem – one of the greatest scientific challenges of the eighteenth century. Not being able to accurately determine longitude had serious implications and was costing a fortune in lives, ships and cargoes lost. This led to the passing of the Longitude Act of 1714, in effect the world's first government-sponsored research and development project with a cash prize of £20,000, equivalent to three million pounds today. John Harrison, born in West Yorkshire, a joiner, self-taught clockmaker and scientist, was inspired by the challenge. He embarked on solving the problem, convinced that precision time-keeping was the route to success.

Harrison devised methods to stop his clocks losing time, inventing along the way the bimetallic strip seen today in every household kettle. He achieved an unprecedented accuracy of one second a month with this clock – making it, in 1727, the most accurate clock in the world. He named it 'Precision-pendulum Clock No. 2'. It is signed by John's younger brother, James Harrison, a skilled carpenter with whom he worked for a time. The technology to keep accurate time now mastered, Harrison made further refinements and portable versions until the sea watch H4, which was eventually recognised as the winning solution to the problem of determining longitude at sea.

In the early 1970s, at a dinner at 10 Downing Street, Neil Armstrong proposed a toast to John Harrison. His invention, Armstrong said, enabled men to explore the Earth with precision and, when most of the Earth had been explored, to dare to build navigation systems for voyages to the Moon. He said, 'You, ladies and gentlemen, started us on our trip.'

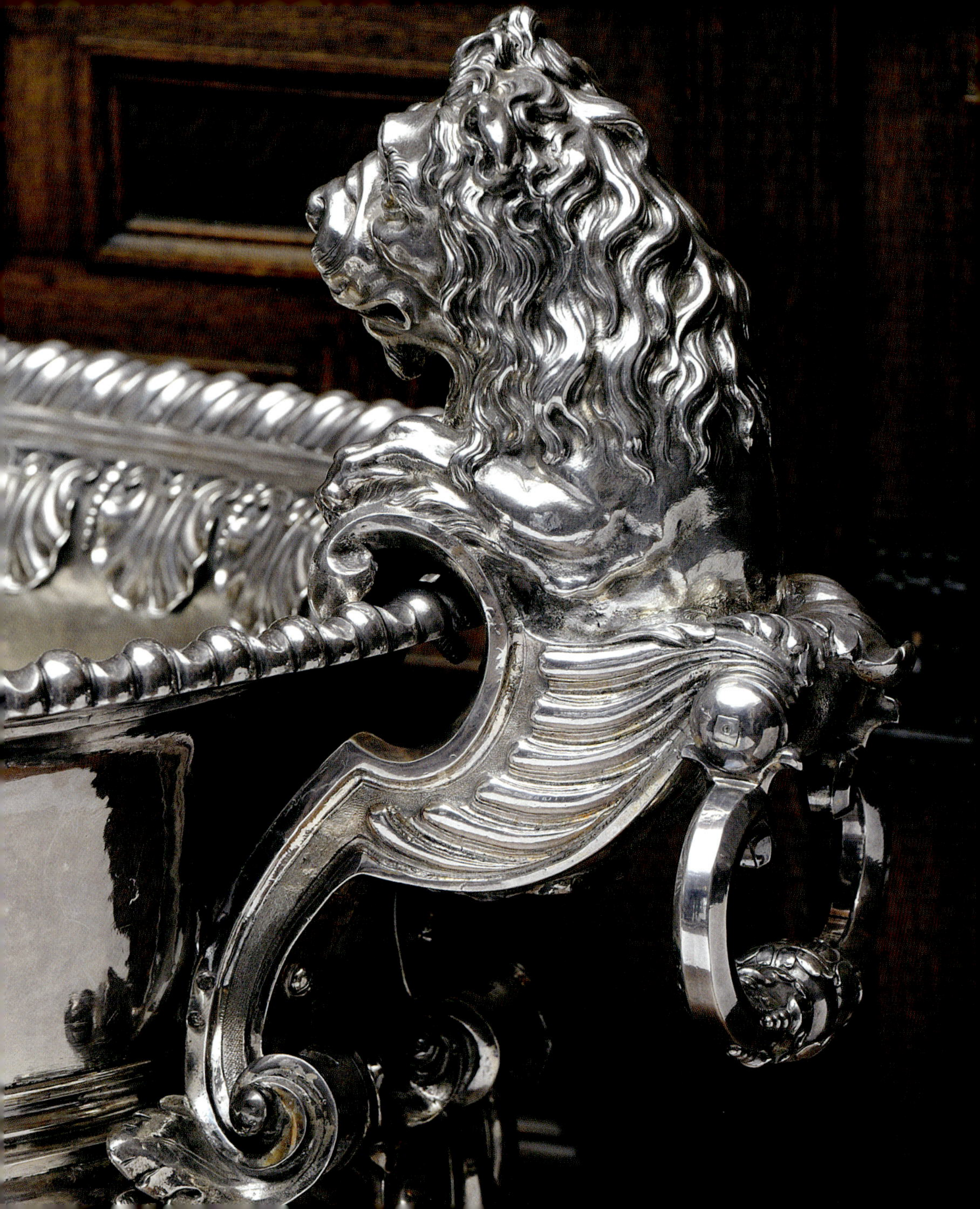

Great silver wine cistern, 1705

Philip Rollos I, active *c.*1685–1710

Silver, 83 × 129.5 cm

Purchase (export license deferral), 2011

LEEAG.2011.322

Continuing the theme of show-stopping objects, this simply enormous wine cooler is the extraordinary feature of the Temple Newsam dining room. In 2011 we were approached to raise funds to save the cooler for the nation following an export licence deferral.

Weighing more than 2,500 ounces and measuring 129.5 cm wide, this wine cistern was granted under the Privy Seal to Thomas Wentworth, 3rd Baron Raby of Wentworth Castle, Yorkshire (later Earl of Stafford). It bears the maker marks of Philip Rollos senior, one of the finest immigrant goldsmiths of the late seventeenth and early eighteenth century. It is engraved with the royal arms and cipher of Queen Anne on the front, attributable to John Rollos, Philip's son.

Lord Raby was appointed ambassador to Berlin in 1705 and as such was entitled to choose objects from the Royal Jewel Office for entertaining in the name of the sovereign. Silver wine cisterns had been used since the sixteenth century to chill wine, but those of this size were intended to catch the eye and emphasise the status of the monarch as much as anything else. This particular cistern would have been displayed in the British Embassy in Berlin during an important time in the history of the English-Brandenburg relationship, as a mark of British culture and competence. It would have been accompanied by other buffet plates including a helmet-shaped ewer and basin by the same maker, both now on display in the British Galleries at the V&A Museum.

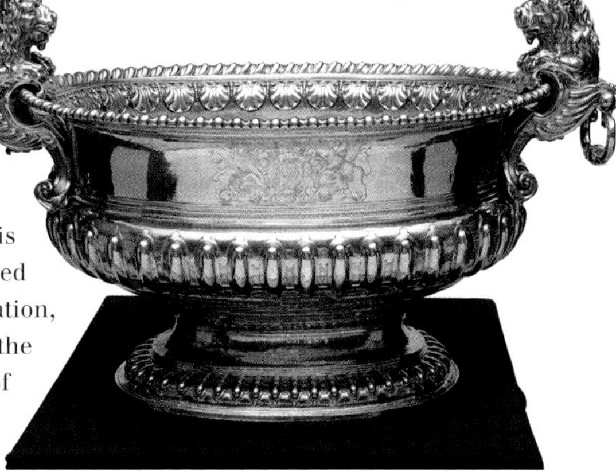

As a feat of engineering and craftsmanship it is surely unrivalled. Its proportions are carefully calculated to balance the weight with the elegance of the decoration, and close inspection reveals the substantial nature of the solder joints and rivets. A truly remarkable piece of silverwork which never fails to turn heads whenever anyone enters the dining room at Temple Newsam.

Lady Muncaster's workbox, 1828

Charles Reilly and George Storer

Ebony, silver, mother of pearl, velvet, 16 × 35 × 34.5 cm

Purchased, 2012

LEEAG.2012.472

A very recent acquisition for Temple Newsam is this exceptionally fine and complete example of a Regency workbox. It comes complete with everything a refined lady would require for her needlework, regarded at the time as one of the most highly esteemed of female accomplishments. We have very few items of such a personal nature belonging to the women of a house, making this a prized and unique treasure. It was made for the marriage, on 15 December 1828, of Frances Catherine Ramsden, granddaughter of Charles and Frances Ingram, last Viscount and Viscountess Irwin of Temple Newsam, to Lowther Augustus John, 3rd Baron Muncaster.

After the death of the ninth and last Viscount Irwin in 1778 Temple Newsam became very much a woman's domain. His widow lived until 1807, being succeeded by two of their five daughters. Frances Catherine's mother, Louisa Susanna, lived some five miles from Temple Newsam and was a frequent visitor. Louisa's sisters (Frances Catherine's aunts) were women of character, determination and style. The eldest, Lady Hertford, was George IV's closest confidante for 12 years; the second, Lady William Gordon, was a well-known philanthropist; and Harriet Aston was lady-in-waiting to the Princess of Wales and married to a celebrated sportsman. To have an item of such a personal nature and of such exquisite quality brings the ladies of the Temple Newsam household vividly to life.

Since the house became a museum in 1938, successive curators have worked tirelessly to build the Designated Collection of decorative arts. The house contents were dispersed in 1922 at the time the estate was purchased by the city from the Honourable Edward Wood (later Earl of Halifax), and subsequent decades have returned many of the original treasures to the house.

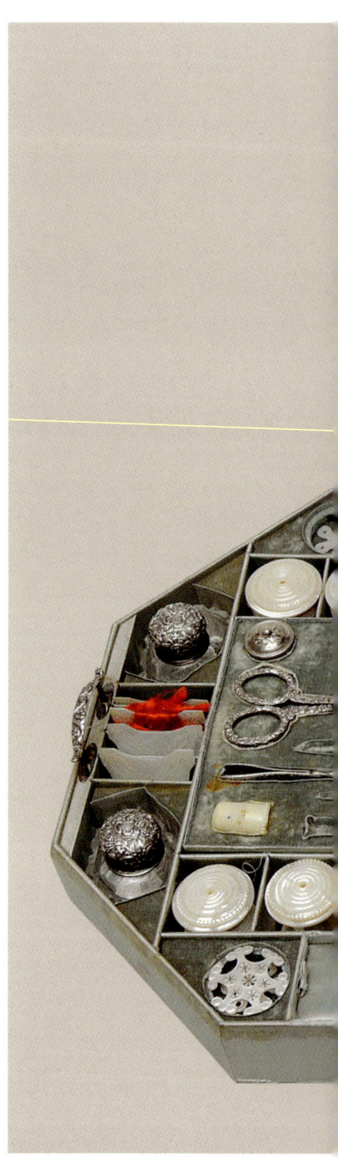

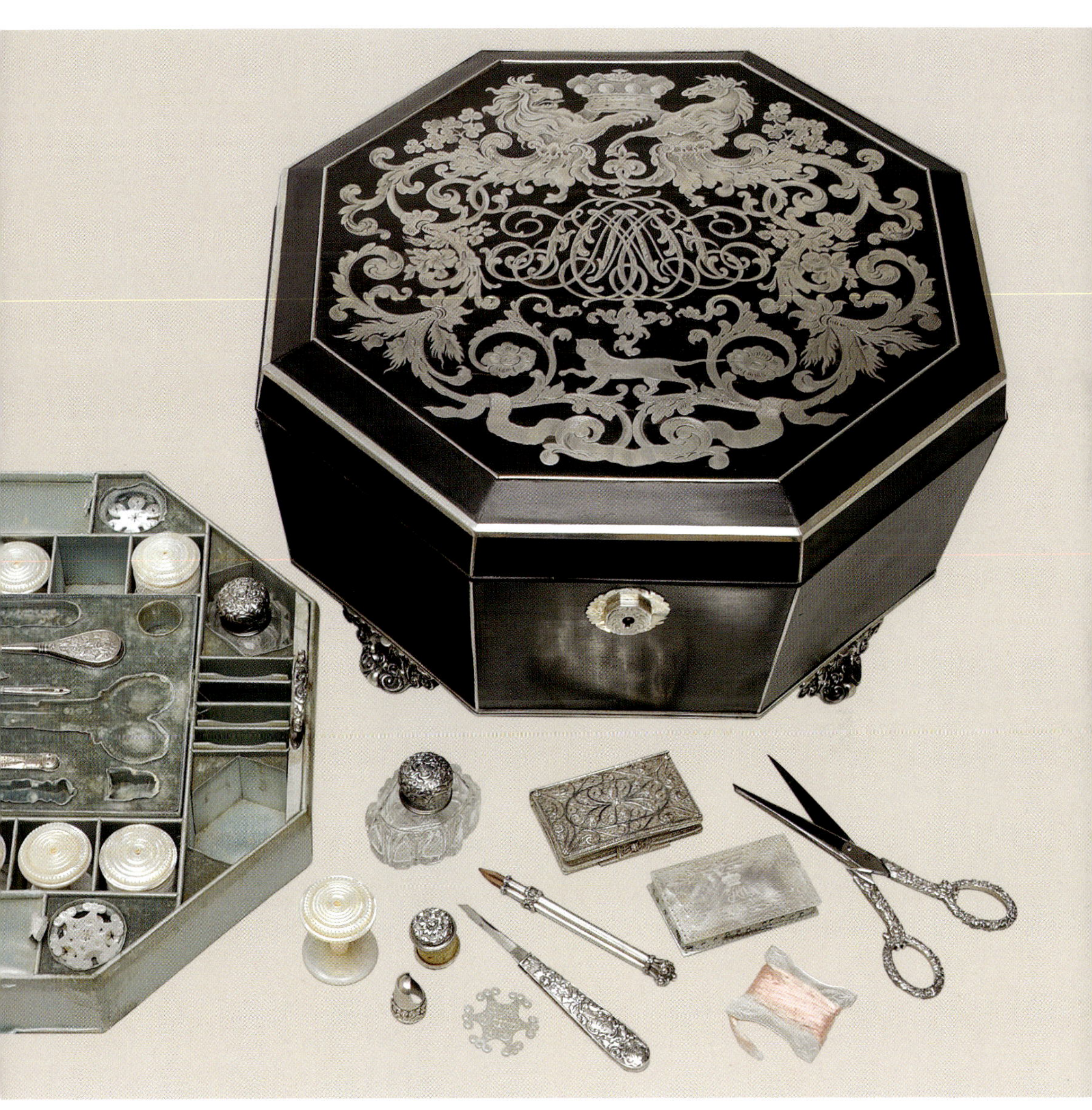

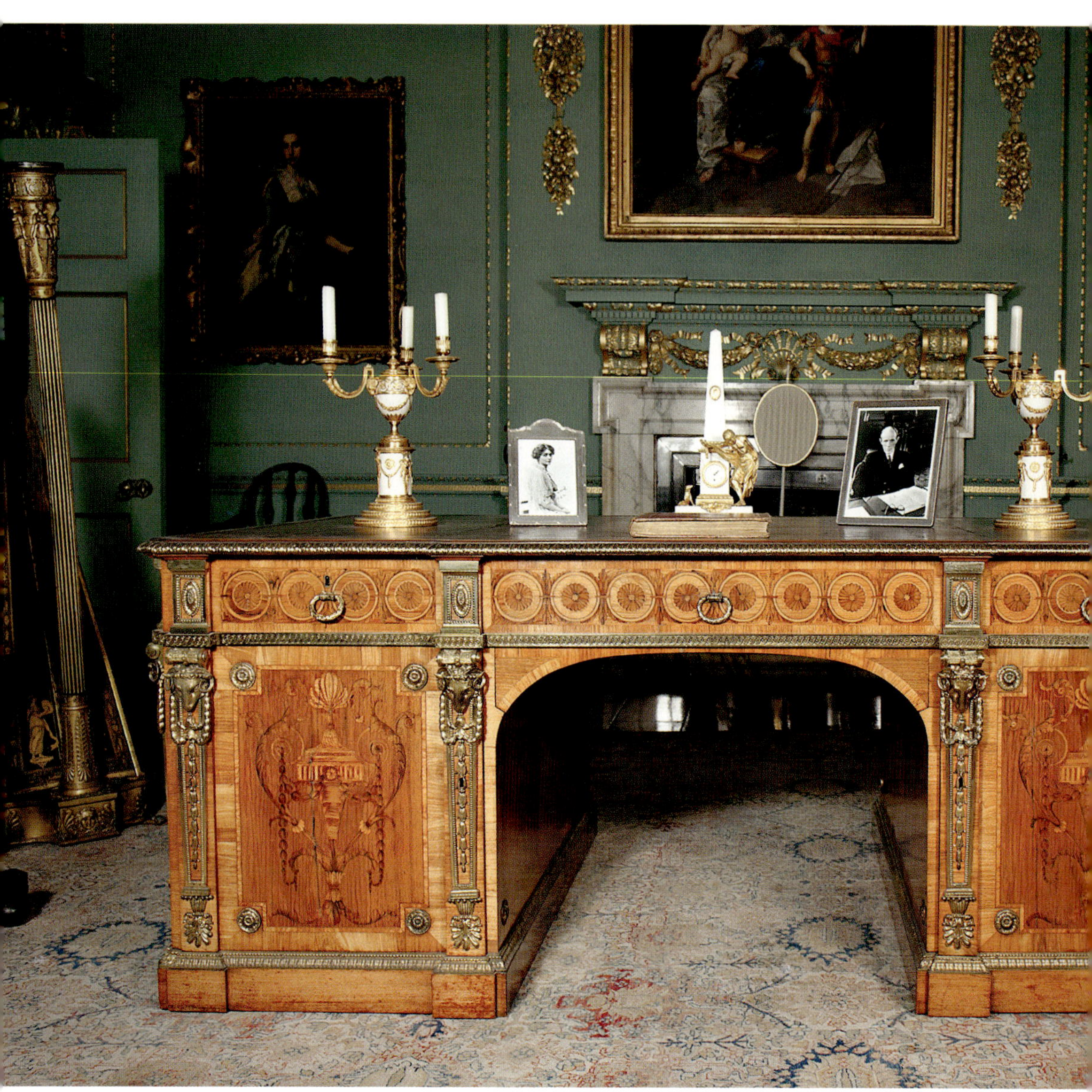

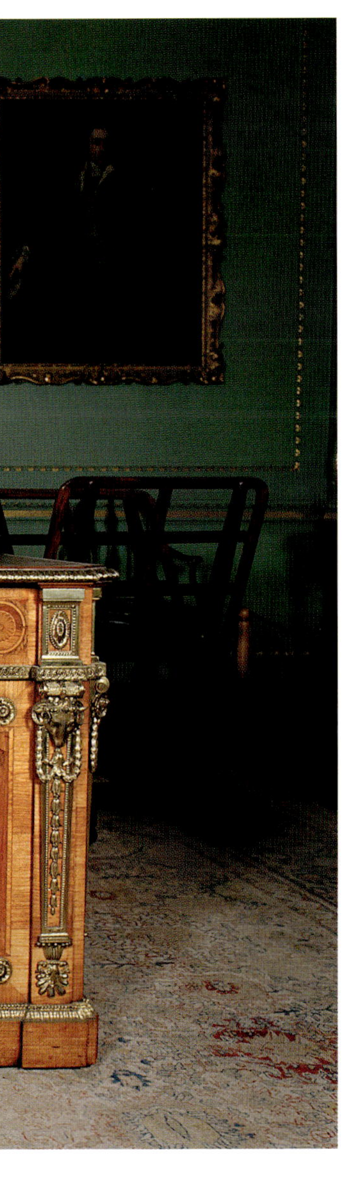

Harewood writing table, c.1771

THOMAS CHIPPENDALE, 1718–1778

Rosewood, oak, pine, mahogany, beech, tulipwood, satinwood, sycamore, holly and various woods,

84 × 207 × 120 cm

Purchased at Christies auction, 1965

LEEAG.FU.1965.21

TEMPLE NEWSAM'S CLAIM to be the 'Hampton Court of the North' is easy to see in its fine Tudor-Jacobean architecture and splendid surroundings. There has been a dwelling on the site for almost a thousand years, originally a property of the Knights Templar and then hugely extended by Lord Darcy in 1520. Its royal claim to fame is that it was the birthplace of Lord Darnley in 1545 and ever since it has been a hub of aristocratic life. However, its reputation as one of the great English historic houses is surely borne out through the range and quality of its collection of fine and decorative arts. The collections of furniture, silver, ceramics, textiles and wallpapers span 500 years and contain some of the most outstanding examples of English craftsmanship seen anywhere.

Of particular note is the collection of furniture made by the renowned furniture maker and designer Thomas Chippendale, who was born 14 miles away in Otley in 1718. Our own collection of his furniture and designs, augmented by those of the Chippendale Society, which are on permanent loan to Temple Newsam, showcase the range and genius of his work.

One of his early neo-classical masterpieces is the library writing table made for Robert Adam's magnificent palace at Harewood House around 1771. Almost architectural in design and intended as the centrepiece of a room, the table is decorated in the most exquisite marquetry, which was returning to vogue at the time, with imagery and ornamentation in a lavish variety of timbers. The table remained at Harewood, passing through the generations, until 1965 when the 7th Earl of Harewood entered it into the Christie's sale and Leeds Corporation secured it with the aid of local benefactors and the National Art Collections Fund.

pp. 10/11: Bought with the aid of a grant from the V&A Purchase Grant Fund.
p. 19: Purchased with the aid of grants from the National Heritage Memorial Fund, The Art Fund, West Yorkshire Grants and the Leeds Art Fund.
pp. 46/47: Bought with the aid of grants from the National Heritage Memorial Fund, The Art Fund, The Wolfson Foundation, The Headley Trust, Leeds Philosophical and Literary Society, Friends of Leeds City Museums and The Goldsmiths' Company.
pp. 62/63: Purchased with the aid of the V&A Purchase Grant Fund.
pp. 74/75: Purchased with the aid of grants from the National Heritage Memorial Fund, the Art Fund, the Monument Trust, the J Paul Getty Jnr Charitable Trust and the Leeds Art Fund.
pp. 76/77: Purchased with the aid of the Leeds Art Fund.
pp. 78/79: Purchased with the aid of The Art Fund.

First published in 2014 by
Scala Arts & Heritage Publishers Ltd
21 Queen Anne's Gate
London SW1H 9BU
www.scalapublishers.com

In association with Leeds Museums and Galleries
www.leeds.gov.uk/museumsandgalleries

ISBN: 978 1 85759 840 7 (museums edition)
ISBN: 978 1 85759 898 8 (galleries edition)

Editor: Sandra Pisano
Text editor for Leeds Museums and Galleries: Camilla Nichol
Design: Nigel Soper
Printed in Singapore

10 9 8 7 6 5 4 3 2 1

FRONT COVER (MUSEUMS EDITION):
John Atkinson Grimshaw,
Park Row, Leeds (see pp. 24/25)

BACK COVER (MUSEUMS EDITION):
The West Yorkshire Hoard
(see pp. 46/47)

FRONT COVER (GALLERIES EDITION):
Percy Wyndham Lewis,
Praxitella (see pp. 12/13)

BACK COVER (GALLERIES EDITION):
Chinese silk banyan, detail
(see pp. 58/59)

FRONTISPIECE:
Great silver wine cistern
(see pp. 74/75)